"Quintessential Brueggemann! He has one screen open to the Bible, another to the broader culture, and a third screen open to developing theories in the fields such as economics and sociology. And he has the sound up to eleven on all the screens at once. Yet in the cacophony, Brueggemann hears the word of God and proclaims it with articulate faith and reverent humility."

—ROLF JACOBSON
Professor of Old Testament, Luther Seminary

"Walter Brueggemann exhorts us to take seriously the power of our words and to be brave in our use of language that is world-creating and prophetically imaginative. The peculiar and relational dialect of the church should empower, not embarrass, us to give enlivened expression of the steadfast and tenacious love of God. We have been deputized to speak in a new tongue!"

—CLOVER REUTER BEAL
Co-lead pastor, Montview Blvd Presbyterian Church

"Among biblical interpreters, Walter Brueggemann is a singular wordsmith. His luminous essays in *The Peculiar Dialect of Faith* explore biblical words in their literary settings and historical conditioning to expose the language worlds they create. Brueggemann refuses to leave these poetic worlds in the past or to wield them as weapons against the present. Instead, his powerful words about texts embrace readers of faith, draw us to full attention, expand our understanding, and call us to renewed hope amid throbbing sufferings of our present moment."

—KATHLEEN M. O'CONNOR
Professor emerita of Old Testament, Columbia Theological Seminary

THE PECULIAR DIALECT OF FAITH

THE PECULIAR DIALECT
OF FAITH

—And Other Essays—

Walter Brueggemann

CASCADE *Books* • Eugene, Oregon

THE PECULIAR DIALECT OF FAITH
And Other Essays

Cascade Books
An Imprint of Wipf and Stock Publishers
199 W. 8th Ave., Suite 3
Eugene, OR 97401

www.wipfandstock.com

PAPERBACK ISBN: 978-1-6667-1517-0
HARDCOVER ISBN: 978-1-6667-1518-7
EBOOK ISBN: 978-1-6667-1519-4

Cataloging-in-Publication data:

Names: Brueggemann, Walter, author.

Title: The peculiar dialect of faith : and other essays / Walter Brueggemann.

Description: Eugene, OR: Cascade Books, 2023. | Includes bibliographical references and index.

Identifiers: ISBN: 978-1-6667-1517-0 (paperback). | ISBN: 978-1-6667-1518-7 (hardcover). | ISBN: 978-1-6667-1519-4 (ebook).

Subjects: LCSH: Bible—Criticism, interpretation, etc. | Bible—Hermeneutics. | Church and social problems.

Classification: BS1192.5 B825 2023 (print). | BS1192.5 (epub).

CONTENTS

PREFACE

I AM FULLY CONVINCED that the Bible teems with contemporaneity for the church. That is, it is what the Spirit speaks to the church. It is for that reason that in all of my work I seek to let the biblical text interact with our currently lived reality. This interaction calls to mind the old saw (often attributed to Karl Barth) about "The Bible in one hand and the newspaper in the other." Such interaction makes it possible for the Bible to help us read contemporary reality differently, as though the God of the Gospel were a real character and a lively agent in the life of the world. More surprising, attention to current social reality also helps us to read the Bible more knowingly, because the Bible is never read in a vacuum; it is always read and interpreted in a context that pushes the interpreter (preacher, teacher) in some imaginative direction.

The interaction between the two, however, is seldom obvious or straightforward. That is, the Bible does not serve either to *predict* or to *prove* anything in our contemporary social reality. The interface between the two is much more impressionistic than it is direct. Thus to appreciate the interface we must to some extent be prepared to proceed by image, figure, and poetic claim, because the connections are rarely exact. In these several pieces I hope I have made fully evident the way in which such impressionistic imagination can bear rich interpretive fruit. Much of the trouble the church has created for itself arises from a misunderstanding of this point and the consequent disregard we practice with reference to the nature of our articulation.

The lead essay on "Peculiar Dialect" (that gives us the title for the collection) is an insistence that the Bible is cast, for the most part, in an idiom that refuses and contends with the hegemonic language of power and certitude. Biblical utterance, in contrast to the rhetoric of power and certitude, offers imaginative probes into the mystery of God's creation and into the hidden complexities of human hurt and human hope. Thus the dialect of the Bible is offered in relational terms, so that the key ingredients to lived reality characteristically concern justice and righteousness, steadfast love, faithfulness, and compassion. Insofar as the church relies upon and attests to this dialect, we may expect that in church we will speak in a different rhetoric and, consequently, we will speak about different subject matter.

To be sure, the church is sometimes seduced away from this relational dialect to speak in cadences that are elementally alien to the Bible and to the claims of the gospel. Such seduction of the church takes place, for example, when our nation is at war and the church is tempted to reflect and reiterate the force of that social reality. Or such seduction occurs when the church is captured by any *ism*, notably in our time, *racism* or *nationalism*. Or alternatively, the church is lured into ideological *conservatism* that craves the language of certitude or ideological *liberalism* that is easily bewitched by the rhetoric of psychology or the market. When the church is domesticated to such alien claims, it loses its distinctiveness and its nerve and its courage for serious mission. Thus attentiveness to our peculiar dialect is an important investment.

My favorite piece in this collection is the one titled "The Protocols of Scarcity." It is my favorite because it permits me to explore the interface between biblical faith and the economic realities of our society. It is to be recognized at the outset that "economics" is an obscure study, open to easy mystification. It is my hope and my assumption that in this essay I have been able to show, all of the complexities and specificities of economics notwithstanding, that we know enough from the Bible to be active, responsible participants in a serious conversation about the economy. In doing so, we are of course aware that early on Moses led a vigorous labor movement among the powerless who departed from and refused their servitude as "cheap labor" (Exodus 5). We know, moreover, that Jesus got himself executed by the state for his restorative, rehabilitative work among the nobodies of his society. Both Moses and Jesus violated the protocols of their dominant societies. The notion of "protocols" refers to the tacit rules of conduct that are never spelled out, but that are rigorously enforced in informal ways and regularly confirmed, and readily embraced by those who want to "succeed."

It occurs to me that a return to our "peculiar dialect" in our language of faith, and a recognition of "the protocols of scarcity" taken together invite the community of faith to speak differently about different subjects in a way that is inherently subversive in the world governed by those protocols. This is what the biblical tradition, from Moses to Jesus, has done without fail. And between Moses and Jesus there is the provocative prophetic movement in ancient Israel that spoke in irascible poetry that the powers of the day found to be unbearably subversive (see Amos 7:10–17). Thus the church has good work to do in order that we ourselves may know the dialect. We may then be prepared to decide together that our witness insists upon the difference that our faith makes in the practical realities of our society.

It is my hope that this collection will help the church and its leaders as the church faces very hard times in our society. Our time requires a ready embrace of a peculiar language that speaks a different version of the world rooted in a different memory that is saturated with gift and wonder.

It remains for me to acknowledge in gratitude those who have made this collection possible. These several pieces first appeared as blogs on the platform, *church.anew* that is directed by Mary Brown. Mary has been vigilantly receptive to my submissions to her, and I am abidingly grateful to her. K. C. Hanson, editor in chief at Wipf and Stock, is graciously receptive to my work and willing to do the hard work that has moved my reflections toward this book form. Finally, Tia Brueggemann has diligently helped my work along, editing my words and engaging in conversation with me about the subject matter. On all counts I am grateful to these generous folk.

I intend this collection to be an act of solidarity with church leaders, pastors, and teachers, in the hope that what I have written will be a useful resource for the hard days of ministry and mission that we may now face.

Walter Brueggemann
Columbia Theological Seminary
January 26, 2023

1

THE PECULIAR DIALECT OF FAITH

IT IS A PRIMARY task of church leadership, in the face of the language of commoditized instrumentalism, to keep alive the peculiar relational, covenantal language of faith. That is, to assure that our peculiar rhetoric remains available and compelling. Given that task, I was somewhat "woke" by this remarkable statement:

A language is a dialect with an army and a navy.[1]

The statement is a recognition of the force of *Realpolitik*. It is an acknowledgement that a hegemonic power can impose its language on other populations in order to advance commercial, military, and cultural domination. A result of such imposition is that vulnerable local and indigenous languages (and cultures) are made marginal for social interaction. The gain is that local populations with different languages are able to communicate with each other in the language of the imposing power, but most often to the benefit of the hegemonic power.

The tag-phrase for such hegemonic language is *lingua franca*, a phrase fashioned in the Middle Ages in the wake of the hegemonic power of Charlemagne. The phrase recognizes that with

1. The statement is attributed, perhaps erroneously, to Max Weinreich by Cagaptay, *Erdogan's Empire*, 121.

1

domination by French power, French became the language of trade and international governance and commerce. But, of course, the phrase has remained useful when the hegemonic language was no longer French with the waning of French domination. In more recent time, of course, English has been the *lingua franca*, first of the British Empire and then with the hegemonic force of the United States. In all of these several variations the *lingua franca* has served well for commerce and the production of wealth for the governing power and its allies. The imposition of such a dominant language has come along with "an army and a navy" to assure domination. At the same time, perhaps inevitably, the dominant language has run roughshod over local language and therefore local culture and local custom. We are most immediately aware of such domination of hegemonic power by the way in which English-speaking nationalism has been intolerant of other languages and cultures in the United States, so that white nationalism has insisted that various immigrant communities must speak English and eschew their mother tongues. In Canada the force of English speaking, with the shameful collusion of the church, has suppressed local language and culture in the most abusive ways.

In the Bible *the great narrative of hegemonic language* is the account of the Tower of Babel (Gen 11:1–9). In that narrative the creator God is alarmed at the imposition of a single language:

> And YHWH said, "Look, they are one people, and they have all one language; and this is only the beginning of what they will do; nothing that they propose to do will now be impossible for them." (v. 6)

Evidently the domination of a single language (and therefore a single culture) generates limitless possibility for economic aggrandizement and political domination. God's response to that hegemonic ambition is to "scatter" and to break up the imposed unity:

> "Come, let us go down, and confuse their language there, so that they will not understand one another's speech." So YHWH scattered them abroad from there over the face of all the earth, and they left off building the city. (vv. 7–8)

Bernhard Anderson has rightly seen the implication of the action of the creator in the narrative:

> The Babel story has profound significance for a biblical theology of pluralism. First, God's will for his creation is diversity rather than homogeneity. We should welcome ethnic pluralism as a divine blessing . . . they are driven, like the builders of Babel, by a creative desire for material glory and fame and a corresponding fear of becoming restless, rootless wanderers.[2]

The outcome of the narrative is refusal of hegemonic power and an affirmation of local variation in language and culture. That outcome, of course, is often linked as an anticipation of the narrative of Pentecost that celebrates linguistic pluralism:

> At this sound the crowd gathered and was bewildered, because each one heard them speaking in the native language of each . . . All were amazed and perplexed, saying to one another, "What does this mean?" (Acts 2:6, 12)

Beyond this foundational narrative of Babel we might consider as well the remarkable interaction between King Hezekiah and the Assyrian ambassador (Rabshakeh) who threatens the king and his city. The Assyrian ambassador (sustained by a mighty military force!) mocks the weak power of King Hezekiah and anticipates the defeat of Hezekiah:

> On what do you base this confidence of yours? Do you think that mere words are strategy and power for war? On whom do you now rely, that you have rebelled against me? See, you are relying now on Egypt, that broken reed of a staff, which will pierce the hand of anyone who leans on it. Such is Pharaoh king Egypt to all who rely on him. But if you say to me, "We rely on YHWH our God, is it not he whose high places and altars Hezekiah removed?" (2 Kgs 18:19–22)

Neither Egypt nor YHWH is seen by the Assyrian as a reliable resource for the king. Neither is a match for Assyria, its army, and its

---

2. Anderson, *From Creation to New Creation*, 177.

gods. The ambassador claims, moreover, that it is none other than YHWH, the God of Israel, who has dispatched the Assyrian army against the city (v. 25). The king's representative, Eliakim, can make no substantive response to the Assyrian mocking. Instead he asks that their parley be conducted in Aramaic, the *lingua franca* of the time, a language not understood by the populace of Jerusalem. Eliakim does not want the king's subjects to be intimidated by the threat of Assyria:

> Please speak to your servants in the Aramaic language, for we understand it; do not speak to us in the language of Judah within the hearing of the people who are on the wall. (v. 26)

But the ambassador refuses and continues in Hebrew, the language of the populace:

> Then the Rabshakeh stood and called out in a loud voice in the language of Judah. (v. 28)

This is a remarkable case in which the hegemonic power dares to utilize local language and refuses the *lingua franca* precisely in order to intimidate more effectively the populace of Jerusalem. Imperial Assyria is not against use of the local language and will use it in its own way to its own advantage.

We may add a wee note from the New Testament. In Matthew's account of the trial of Jesus, Peter is a bystander and a witness, but he wants to remain safe and unrecognized. But his dialect gives him away:

> Another servant-girl saw him, and she said to the bystanders, "This man was with Jesus of Nazareth." Again he denied it with an oath, "I do not know the man." After a little while the bystanders came up and said to Peter, "Certainly you are also one of them, for your accent betrays you." (Matt 26:71–73)

The exchange is between Jews in Jerusalem and Peter from Galilee, so the encounter does not pertain immediately to the Roman Empire and its imperial language. But even the linguistic distinction between a Jerusalem Jew and a Galilean Jew is enough to put Peter at risk. Jerusalem is in the zone of the Roman "army and navy," whereas Galilee, with its rustic dialect, is a back-water territory. The dialect is enough to jeopardize Peter!

This matter of "dialect with an army and a navy" is of intense interest to us currently in the midst of white nationalism. Such nationalism is impatient with difference and intolerant of "deviant" language or culture. The former president's dismissal of "Mexicans" as "rapists" is enough of a signal to appeal to white nationalists and to all those who want to make white America "great again." That impatient, intolerant exclusivism is at the moment backed by "an army and a navy," thus the incessant parade of military regalia to back it up!

Thus we can see that *lingua franca* is a mixed bag. It makes possible international commerce. It makes workable international scientific research and technological advances. It is at the same time, however, a threat to all that is local. It is deeply enmeshed in power that is connected to a system of wealth that is generous in its rewards and savage in its punishments.

The notion of "a dialect with an army and a navy" is an invitation for us to reflect on the peculiar idiom of faith that is relentless in its local specificity that is resolvedly different from the *lingua franca,* and that is resolutely without "an army and a navy." Whereas the *lingua franca* deals in quotas, formulae, sweeping generalizations, and syllogisms, our peculiar dialect patiently works its way via narratives of specificity.

This peculiar language of our faith comes

- with a *memory* of specific stories that are fully occupied by a God who with active verbs performs acts of creation, judgment, and rescue. Those stories bear imaginative retelling (see Psalm 136);

- with a *vision* of a new world that is hospitable to the weak, vulnerable, and left behind;

- with a *discipline* (disciples!) that is an "easy burden" but that entails the daily enactment of the vision.

This peculiar, distinctive dialect that is a "manger" for the truth (Luther)

- refuses tales of wealth or victory;
- refuses visions of private security and power;
- refuses disciplines that are based in fear, scarcity, and greed.

This is a language that tends to contradict in every way the *lingua franca* because it traffics in neighbors and not commodities, because it affirms that relationships constitute the alternative currency of the future, and because it summons to passionate self-giving and not self-protection. In all its parts, language shows us how not to be "rich in things and poor in soul," but to be "rich in soul even if poor in things."

We may learn a great deal from the work of James C. Scott, a sociologist who exhibits no direct interest in matters theological, but much that may be inferred.[3] It is the large thesis of Scott that communities of vulnerability survive and prosper because they have "hidden transcripts" that articulate the world differently outside the purview of the managers of wealth and power. That transcript must be kept hidden and out of reach of the powerful in order that it not be either *co-opted* or *exterminated* by the force of the dominant narrative. The carriers of this sub-version of reality characteristically have no leverage or visible muscle, no "silver or gold" (Acts 3:6), only the joy and freedom of this different world stitched together by this odd dialect.

Thus it is my thought that the church, in order to maintain its identity and its effective missional life, must have leaders that keep that distinctive dialect alive, available, and credible in the most imaginative ways. Church leaders equip the community for a *sub-version* of reality that is inherently *sub-versive* in relation to the dominant dialect with it army and navy. We do so with intentionality through education, liturgy, and missional action. Effective leadership requires that we be situated and at home in a distinctive dialect that does not lust after a life secured by an army and navy or any of the other tools of domination.

3. Scott, *Weapons of the Weak.*

I suggest that there are two seductions that put our mother tongue at risk. On the one hand, we may be tempted to imagine that our dialect can become the dominant dialect in the public domain. This is the temptation of radical right-wingers (who style themselves as "evangelicals"). In the United States such folk, in the pursuit of control and certitude, seek to establish a gospel dialect as the *lingua franca* in the public square. Such an effort transforms the speech of relational covenanting into control and domination. The inevitable outcome of such an effort is to blunt the radical relationality of the gospel and of the community that performs the gospel.

On the other hand, there is a temptation to let the language of the public domain seep into the rhetoric of the church so that the church becomes an echo of public discourse or, more specifically, an echo of *The New York Times*. This is the seduction of progressives in their pursuit of respectability among the "cultured despisers of religion." The effect of such accommodation is the loss of the sharp critical edge of the missional life of the church in its capacity to challenge dominant culture in significant ways.

Both of these seductions, one greedily ambitious and the other hopelessly accommodating, cause serious gospel identity to be eroded. In both instances the gospel is seriously distorted. Church leaders may usefully reflect on how urgent is the peculiar relational insistence of our faith amid a society that wants to reduce everything and everyone to a tradable commodity. Our relational dialect is a bold counter-insistence that our common life cannot be reduced to such transactions because God has intended from the outset that we be a community of neighbors, a claim definitional for both our talk and our walk. We are familiar with the shorthand mantras that mark our talk, for example:

- Full of grace and truth
- Faith, hope, and love, these three
- Justice and righteousness
- Trust and obey
- Grace and glory.

The work is to show how these familiar phrasings are stitched together into a credible coherence that gives us a place to stand, with freedom and courage, amid a larger language dependent on army and navy that can never be the parlance of the coming Kingdom of God.

2

THE DUTY AND THE DESTINY
OF A SHOVELER

WHAT FOLLOWS HERE IS an act of self-indulgence. It is not likely to
be informative, instructive, or edifying for you, dear reader. Thus
you may desist from reading further. I have written this simply
because I wanted to, to see what I could make of a line I have read
recently. The line is from the third volume of the trilogy of Hilary
Mantel on Thomas Cromwell—a wonderful read. Cromwell was
the chief aide to and fixer for Henry VIII. He fixed everything for
the king. He fixed the church as it departed from Rome. He fixed
the dissolution of the monasteries. He broke the back of noble
families that had foolishly crossed the king. And he managed the
coming and going of Henry's first four wives. He was the son of a
lowly blacksmith, but he rose to great power and wealth, becoming
second only to the king in the realm. (He was not unlike Joseph to
Pharaoh in the book of Genesis [Gen 41:40].)

Of Cromwell, Hilary Mantel can write:

> Somewhere—or Nowhere, perhaps—there is a society
> ruled by philosophers. They have clean hands and pure
> hearts. But even in the metropolis of light, there are
> middens [dunghills] and manure-heaps, swarming with

flies. Even in the republic of virtue you need a man who
will shovel up the shit, and somewhere it is written that
Cromwell is his name.[1]

Cromwell is the great shoveler! There was, moreover, plenty to
shovel in Henry's self-indulgent reign. But then, characteristically,
powerful persons need shovelers because almost every powerful
person, short of a society of philosophers, produces plenty of ex-
crement that requires disposal.

This wondrously understated paragraph by Mantel got me to
wondering if I could identify such a shoveler in the Bible. And
sure enough, the nominee is Joab, the shoveler for King David.
Thus in what follows I will explore how and in what ways Joab is
a compelling match for the heavy lifting that Cromwell will do in
his turn for the king. We may identify the shoveling work of Joab
in six distinct episodes.

2 Samuel 3:24–27

Abner, the leader of Saul's continuing northern movement, seeks
to make peace with David. Joab, however, perceives Abner as a
threat to David (and surely a threat to Joab's position as well). Joab
reprimands David for allowing Abner to escape from his grasp
(3:24). But then Joab on his own seeks out Abner and kills him:

> When Abner returned to Hebron, Joab took him aside
> in the gateway to speak with him privately, and there he
> stabbed him in the stomach. So he died for shedding the
> blood of Asahel, Joab's brother. (v. 27)

David does not object to the killing of Abner. He objects that he
might be blamed for the killing and makes sure that Joab receives
the credit/blame for the death of Abner.

---

1. Mantel, *The Mirror and the Light*, 373.

2 Samuel 11:14–21

Joab obeys the instruction of David, putting Uriah forward in battle where he is sure to be killed. By doing this, Joab has rescued David from a most awkward situation concerning the pregnancy of Bathsheba. Joab is confident that David will not worry about the outcome of the battle, but only that Uriah has been eliminated. The king blows off the killing of Uriah without blinking:

> Do not let this matter trouble you, for the sword devours now one and now another. (v. 25)

2 Samuel 14:1–24

Joab perceives that David is preoccupied with his son Absalom, even though Absalom has been banished from the court for the murder of his brother. Joab receives no instruction from the king, but he understands that David will welcome his banished son back into his presence. Joab undertakes a surreptitious initiative so that Absalom might be restored to the king's presence. He choreographs a scene:

> In order to change the course of affairs. (v. 20)

Joab's; choreography works to perfection. When David discerns Joab's hand in the plot for restoration he agrees to it, as though Joab had forced his hand:

> Very well, I grant this; go, bring back the young man Absalom. (v. 21)

Not unlike Cromwell, Joab is careful for himself and bows in obedience to the king, expressing gratitude that the king has accepted his surreptitious aid:

> Joab prostrated himself with his face to the ground and did obeisance, and blessed the king; and Joab said, "To-day your servant knows that I have found favor in your

sight, my lord, the king, that the king has granted the
request of his servant." (v. 22)

2 Samuel 18:1–15

Absalom is in rebellion against his father. The father and son are at
war. Joab is on the hunt for Absalom who is a threat to his father.
Joab is indignant when he learns that Absalom had slipped away
from his men when he might have been killed:

> What, you saw him! Why then did you not strike him he
> to the ground? I would have been glad to give you ten
> pieces of silver and a belt. (v. 11)

But the potential killers of Absalom were reluctant to kill the king's
son (v. 12). Joab, partisan that he is, has no such scruple. He is
single-minded in his devotion to David; he has no reservation
about seeking the death of the king's son. He finds Absalom and
his men kill him:

> And ten young men, Joab's armor-bearers, surrounded
> Absalom and struck him, and killed him. (v. 15)

Beyond the death itself, Joab carefully orchestrates the report
of the death to David, for he knows that the king wanted Absalom
protected even as he rebelled (vv. 19–32; see v. 12). Joab, much
more than David himself, is clear-eyed about the requirements of
monarchy. He will readily act against the reluctance of the king,
and will do what is necessary for the wellbeing of David. He will
not linger over David's sentimental attachment to his son.

2 Samuel 19:1–8

Joab must deal with the king's deep grief over the death of Absalom. The king is seen in public to be smitten with disconsolate grief
over his loss (18:33—19:5). It is as though David has taken a leave
of absence from being king, a sure manifestation of weakness. Joab

will have none of it. He cares not at all about the king's grief. He cares only that David be perceived in public as strong, engaged, and functioning as king. He does not hesitate to rebuke the king for his parental emotion:

> Today you have covered with shame the faces of all your officers who have saved your life today, and the lives of your sons and daughters, and the lives of your wives and your concubines . . . for I perceive that if Absalom were alive and all of us were dead today, then you would be pleased. (vv. 5–6)

Given this reprimand he makes to the king, Joab issues a command to the king that he must appear as a king:

> So go out at once and speak kindly to your servants. (v. 7)

In response to Joab's imperative, David obeys, appears, and assures his troops. By his own lights Joab has saved the king from his debilitating show of vulnerability.

2 Samuel 20:7–10, 20–22

Joab is preoccupied with the challenge to David posed by Sheba, a Benjaminite and perhaps one who continues the claim and threat of the party of Saul in the north. David dispatched one, Amasa, to eliminate the challenge of the rebel from the north. Amasa however delays and misses his appointment. We are not told why he was late, and the narrator does not care. What counts is that the challenge to the king lasted longer than it should have. In response to the delay, Joab, without any mandate from David, acts quickly and decisively:

> Joab took Amasa by the beard with his right hand to kiss him. But Amasa did not notice the sword in Joab's hand; Joab struck him in the belly so that his entrails poured out on the ground, and he died. He did not strike a second blow. (vv. 9–10)

Joab promptly disposes of Amasa and pursues Sheba who posed a threat to David. Joab pauses with a wise woman and declares his reluctance to "swallow up or destroy," but explains why he must act against Sheba. The wise woman understands and accepts Joab's requirement and presents Sheba's head to Joab:

> And they cut off the head of Sheba son of Bichri, and threw it down to Joab. So he blew the trumpet, and they dispersed from the city, and all went to their homes, while Joab returned to Jerusalem to the king. (v. 22)

Having completed his shoveling work, another unblinking protection of the king, Joab returns to home base.

2 Samuel 24:1–9

David initiates a census. In response, Joab issues a generic good wish to his king (v. 3). But then he confronts David with a wonderment as to why the king would want to conduct a census:

> But why does my lord the king want to do this? (v. 3)

Joab recognizes that a census bears marks of bureaucratic control that cannot enhance David in the eyes of his populace (or of YHWH). Joab does not hesitate to question the king. The king does not bother to answer Joab, and Joab promptly moves in obedience to conduct the census. Joab is vigilant for his king, but he will in the end obey the will of the king.

> Joab reported to the king the number of those who had been recorded. (v. 9)

It is astonishing to notice how much of David's narrative is occupied by the action of Joab. Two feature stand out in my reading of the narrative. First, Joab is a killer for the king. He does not hesitate to dispatch and eliminate those who jeopardize David's rule. He executed Abner (3:27), Uriah (11:16–17), Absalom (18:14–15), and Amasa and Sheba (20:9–10, 21–22). This is indeed the work of a faithful shoveler. Never does Joab show any remorse or regret for violent actions. And not once does David commend or thank Joab. It is as if the killings are beyond the ken or intent of the king, even though David surely recognized both the brutality of Joab, and the gains he received from that brutality.

Second, it is remarkable that Joab can frontally question David in aggressive ways. Thus in the case of Abner:

> What have you done? Abner came to you; why did you dismiss him, so that he got away? You know that Abner son of Ner came to deceive you, and learn your comings and goings and to learn all that you are doing. (3:24–25)

In the case of the death of Absalom Joab boldly reprimands David for his show of grief in neglect of his royal work:

> Today you have covered with shame the faces of all your officers who have saved your life today . . . for love of those who hate you and for hatred of those who love you. You have made it clear today that commander and officers are nothing to you. (19:5–6)

And with reference to the census:

> But why does my lord the king want to do this? (24:3)

In each case the narrative exhibits Joab in his mastery of the matter at hand. In the case of Uriah, Joab knows exactly what is up with David; he knows that the good news of the death of Uriah will override any other matter of the battle (11:18–22). In the death of Abner, Joab knows that the king would not object to the killing. In the case of Absalom, he carefully prepares the report to David in a way that protects the son of Zadok the priest, a member of the king's inner circle (18:19–32). In addition to "bringing down the bodies,"[2] Joab manages public relations for the king. He looks after the king's interest even when the king behaves, in his judgment, foolishly and irresponsibly.

It is not difficult to conclude that the success of David is due to the action of Joab in the same way that Henry's success depended on Cromwell. What does the shoveler get for all of his risky, daring

---

2. See Mantel, *Bring Up the Bodies.*

action and attentiveness? After the elimination of Abner, David is most concerned that he will to be blamed for the convenient death. In order to deflect any such notion, David stages an elaborate state funeral for Abner, declaring that "a prince and a great man" has died (3:38). More than that David requires Joab to participate in public grief, surely a profound humiliation for Joab:

> Tear your clothes and put on sackcloth and mourn over Abner. (3:31)

David does not mind humiliating his shoveler. He cares only for own self-protection.

And then, finally, as with many such shovelers, Joab is undone by the son of David. On his deathbed David admonishes his son to eliminate Joab:

> Moreover you know also what Joab son of Zeruiah did to me, how he dealt with the two commanders of the armies of Israel, Abner son of Ner, and Amasa son of Jether . . . Act therefore according to your wisdom, but do not let his gray head go down to Sheol in peace. (1 Kgs 2:5–6)

For the first time Joab miscalculates; he bets on the wrong son of David, Adonijah, as successor to David. As a result, Solomon acts swiftly to eliminate the long-standing shoveler who served "the family" faithfully:

> Strike him down and bury him; and thus take away from me and from my father's house the guilt for the blood that Joab shed without cause. YHWH will bring back his bloody deeds on his own head, because without the knowledge of my father David, he attacked and killed with the sword two men more righteous and better than himself, Abner son of Ner, commander of the army of Israel, and Amasa son of Jether commander of the army of Judah. So shall the blood come back on the head of Joab and on the head of his descendant forever, but to David and to his descendants and to his house and to his throne, there shall be peace from YHWH forevermore. (1 Kgs 2:31–33)

Like his father before him, Solomon is devoted to maintaining for himself and his house the appearance of innocence from any bloodguilt. Indeed, he goes so far as to suggest that both Abner and Amasa are innocent and that Joab is guilty. And, of course, it can be granted in both cases that Joab eliminated a rival. But any claim of innocence is rather belated in this royal family that has gained so much from Joab's ruthless loyalty. But so it goes with shovelers! Like Cromwell, Joab has been absolutely essential for the maintenance of royal power and yet completely dispensable at the right time. And like Cromwell, at the end Joab is disdained and dismissed. The narrator gives us all of this without blinking or explaining or justifying. It is what it is! History makes clear that Joab helped to maintain the "family." At the end, of course, as a son of Zeruiah—like Cromwell, the son of a blacksmith—is not valued by the winners. We get this final note:

> Benaiah son of Jehoiada went up and struck him down
> and killed him; and he was buried at his own house near
> the wilderness. (1 Kgs 2:34)

That's it! A son of Zeruiah, like the English son of a blacksmith, is left dead, not grieved, not thanked.

From this remarkable narrative I will extrapolate only two obvious points. First, this cunning, thick narrative makes clear that Israel's faith was formed and practiced in the world of *Realpolitik*. This cast of characters is calculating, ruthless, and formidable. And they have found a narrator to match their greedy, violent resolve. The point is important because it makes clear that the rootage of Messianism (especially Christian messianism) is in the real world. The expectation of a "New David" who will restore Israel to power is grounded in the remembered David. And while Jesus is saluted as "son of David" (Mark 10:47–48), he does not fit the claim, he does not welcome the claim, and his genealogy does not add up to that. This rootage is an important corrective to any excessively pious reading of "Jesus as the New David. This recognition also suggests that the New Testament, not unlike the Old, is deeply grounded in historical political realism. When Jesus "set his face steadfastly to go to Jerusalem" he surely knew about the dangerous contradiction to Jerusalem political that he was to perform and enact (Luke 9:51). This does not mean he had some secret "foreknowledge," but that he was alert and realistic about the world of power. Paul Lehmann has written wisely and shrewdly about the "transfiguration of politics" and focuses on the conflict of Jesus with Pilate, the imperial governor:

> The political thrust of this participial "lifestyle" is exposed in the confrontation between Jesus and Pilate. The question of the Establishment is up: the question whose world is this, and by what or whose authority. It is understandable that Pilate should have asked Jesus, "Where have you come from?" . . . Pilate's honest perplexity about truth was revealed in his puzzlement that should require truth if it sought to command authority . . . Jesus, on the other hand, affirms, both by conviction and by role, that the only authority power has is the authority of truth.[3]

The David story invites us to ponder the strange vulnerability of power, and the equally strange power that is denied the powerful. If and when politics is transfigured after the manner of Jesus, there will be no need for a shoveler. Imagine!

Second we can readily keep one eye on contemporaneity as we think about the shoveler. If it is true, as it surely is, that powerful people characteristically require a shoveler, then the nominee for shoveler for our former president is undoubtedly Michael Cohen. He was the fixer and shoveler *par excellence* for former President Trump, as he himself asserts. At the end he was, as was Joab, thrown under the bus by his patron. The writer of the David narrative knows about the sad outcome of power that lacks the basis of truth (see John 18:38). The end for Joab, as we have seen, is not good. But consider the end for David as well. His final word to his son and heir is an inventory for vengeance. His final wisdom is "eliminate the threat" (Joab, Shimei) and reward your donor, Barzillai (1 Kgs 2:5–9). This final moment for the king is not one

---

3. Lehmann, *The Transfiguration of Politics*, 55.

of glory, it is one of fear. It is all right to recite the lines attributed to David:

> Even though I walk through the valley of the shadow of
> death,
>> I will fear no evil. (Ps 23:4; author's translation)

Except that David, in his fear, needed a shoveler. And then he did not! Like his master, Joab died in fear:

> When the news came to Joab . . . Joab fled to the tent of
> YHWH and grasped the horns of the altar. (1 Kgs 2:28)

3

THE FORCE OF OWNERSHIP

MY EYE FELL, ACCIDENTALLY and fortuitously, on this innocent-looking text that I had not ever studied:

> Now there was no smith to be found throughout all the land of Israel; for the Philistines said, "The Hebrews must not make sword or spear for themselves"; so all the Israelites went down to the Philistines to sharpen their plowshare, mattocks [pickaxes], axes, or sickles. The charge was two-thirds of a shekel for the plowshare and for the mattocks, and one-third of a shekel for sharpening the axes and for setting the goads. So on the day of the battle neither sword nor spear was to be found in the possession of any of the people with Saul and Jonathan; but Saul and his son Jonathan had them. (1 Sam 13:19–22)

At first glance the paragraph seems like a straight-forward historical report. At the most it suggests that the boisterous claim of the book of Joshua that Israel, in its "conquest," had eliminated all the resident population is overblown. That claim is that Joshua had driven out all the "Canaanites," a term that is culturally generic. Here, however, we are told that it is not the Canaanites, but the Philistines who are still in the land. Unlike the "Canaanites," the Philistines are an historically identifiable people, "the Sea Peoples," who arrived in the land at roughly the same time as did the Joshua movement of Israel. The text suggests that the Philistines had stronger economic and military leverage that made the Israelites vulnerable and in many ways dependent upon and subservient to the Philistines. This social distance between these two populations is indicated, moreover, by the reference to Israel, attributed to the Philistines as "Hebrews." The latter term is derogatory and suggests that the Israelites were the undifferentiated "other" of the Philistine "we."

This unequal distinction, moreover, is the primary point of this odd paragraph. It is asserted that the Philistines owned and operated all the blacksmith shops in the land. Israel was not permitted, by the Philistines, to have any forge of anvil or any means by which they might make agricultural or military equipment. The Philistines owned it all. As a result, Israelite farmers had to get their farm equipment such as a sickle or an axe serviced, as required, by the Philistines. The reference to costs in v. 20 suggests both that such service was expensive and that it was arbitrary. And if agricultural equipment was carefully controlled, so was military equipment, an arrangement that left Israel vulnerable and defenseless.

What interests me in this brief text is that it bears witness to the "force of ownership." The Philistines owned and therefore controlled everything that pertained to the practical agricultural life of Israel. And because Israel controlled none of the means to advance its own agricultural or military capacity, Israel was indeed "second class," sure to be dismissed as "Hebrews."

The thesis that I want to pursue here concerns the "force of ownership" and he vulnerable dependence of not being an "owner":

—*Consider:* We are accustomed to (and weary of) hearing that Jeff Bezos, Warren Buffett, and the Walton family control a very high percentage of the wealth of our economy. (Indeed on a recent day it was reported that in a single day Bezos gained thirteen billion dollars while his Amazon workers are in protest over poor working conditions and inadequate pay.) The counterpoint that goes with such a report is that a huge portion of our population owns nothing, controls nothing, and is left precarious and vulnerable. Buffett in his generous honesty could shrewdly observe, "There is a class war and my class is winning." Buffett has elsewhere commented on the inequity of the tax code from which he benefits greatly. The huge population denied ownership is often dismissed in common discourse as "the poor" who are left behind and who are, in many cases, Blacks who are left with the legacy of slavery. Indeed the "planters" of the old plantation system are an iconic representation of the ownership class that controls the political process and who do no work but lived out the great American dream of property based on cheap labor.

—*Consider*: My friend Peter Block reports to me that in the entire United States, there are not many more than twenty gas stations owned by Black persons. We may take this small number, give or take a few, as emblematic of the way in which Black persons, with important exceptions, have been excluded from ownership and consequently excluded from any significant role in the political process. In the plantation economy after emancipation, it was the owners who set the price of cotton for the tenants (not unlike the Philistines set the price!), so that the tenant could be denied income in exploitative ways.

—*Consider*: Martin Caparros, *Hunger: The Oldest Problem*, has fully and carefully characterized the "Other World" that lies outside the benefits of the dominant system of the world economy:

> In the Other World, there are no solid houses, no sewers, no hospitals or schools that cure or teach, no dignified work, no protective state, no guarantees, no future. In the Other World there is not enough food for everybody. This, above all.[1]

Among the matters Caparros hones in on is the strange yet undeniable fact that Monsanto, the aggressive chemical company, has sold its genetically modified seed to farmers in the "Other World," but has *retained ownership* of the seed. It is all about ownership!

1. Caparros, *Hunger: The Oldest Problem*, 93.

Men and women were discussing whether Monsanto, the American agrochemical and agricultural biotechnology company, had the right to the intellectual property of seeds, and one man said no, because Monsanto is a corporation and a corporation is not a person with a mind that can produce intellectual property, and so on.[2]

The most important impact of this new arrangement with Monsanto is a drastic change in social reality among the vulnerable poor:

> Everything changed here [in India] with the arrival of the multinationals like Monsanto, with their seeds and their hunger for more and more land. Before, the government gave land to the peasants; after 1991 they started taking it away from them. And in the meantime, Monsanto was carrying out campaigns in every village in India; they'd arrive in a truck and promise millions to the poor if they started using their seeds. So the farmers bought them, and the whole package along with them; pesticides, fertilizers, the obligation to buy from them again for the next planting. And above all, the peasants focused on growing for the market; everything was cotton, wheat, corn . . . now even soy. Here, the most critical element was the change in mentality: from working to eat to working to swell.[3]

Caparros further comments:

> The private ownership of production is a major contemporary invention. It is a brutal form of the idea of ownership, not of the field, not of the product of the field, but rather of a natural model—the seed—that only its "owner" has the right to produce. Intellectual property rights over nature . . . Within this system technological progress becomes an opportunity for a select few to accumulate more wealth rather than an effort to improve lives.[4]

2. Caparros, *Hunger: The Oldest Problem*, 145.
3. Caparros, *Hunger: The Oldest Problem*, 145–46.
4. Caparros, *Hunger: The Oldest Problem*, 149.

That reality leads to this awareness:

> Whoever controls the design of the seed also controls, in
> some ways, the use of the plant that will grow from that
> seed, that is, the fate of those foodstuffs.[5]

Such political reality must evoke in the Other World that is without leverage, resistance:

> The goal, then, is to invent the way to take control of
> these new technologies, find the political structure to put
> these technologies to work to benefit the many—because
> without these technologies, many millions will have
> problems feeding themselves.[6]

Caparros is careful not to be a Luddite about these newer conditions of food. He sees, rather, that this is an urgent matter of ownership!

I suggest that the "crises of ownership" is already evident in the paragraph of First Samuel. It is at the heart of our ideological debates concerning the economy. The ownership class in the United States, of which I am a member, has comforted itself with the notion that its property (ownership) is the result of industry, frugality, and hard work. Such an illusion disregards the clear reality that this wealth is based on cheap labor and the cheapest of all cheap labor, slavery.

The ownership class knows the price of everything. It is accustomed to buying, selling, and acquiring; consequently, it pays great attention to prices; and not unlike the Philistines, that class sets the price of commodities. But that same ownership class very often does not know the cost of things, because it has not paid the cost. The matter is clear in an episode in the Jesus narrative. Jesus is at a dinner party; a woman comes in and pours olive oil to anoint his feet (Mark 14:3–8). "Some" opposed such a wasteful use of the oil:

---

5. Caparros, *Hunger: The Oldest Problem*, 149.
6. Caparros, *Hunger: The Oldest Problem*, 152.

Why was this ointment wasted in this way? For this ointment could have been sold for more than three hundred
denarii, and the money given to the poor." (vv.4–5)

In Matthew's version it is "the disciples" who make the protest
(Matt 26:8–9). In the Fourth Gospel rendering it is the calculating
Judas (John 12:4–5). In all three versions, it is a question posed by
those who know the price of oil and the price of bread and are able
to do the numbers, and can convert money for relief of the poor.
What they do not know is the force of the oil beyond commodity
pricing. They had no clue about any other value of the oil; they
had no understanding of its sacramental force. They never guessed
about the costliness of his death that the anointing anticipates or
the relational gesture made by the woman. They missed out on the
costliness of what happened because they were fixed on the *price*
of things.

It will be important for the church and its leaders to pay close
and continuing attention to the ownership crisis and the great cost,
for many poor people and people of color, of being excluded from
ownership. After the end of slavery, ownership society has found
many ways of continuing such exclusion, by poll tax (and now
voter repression), by zoning, by leveraged bank loans and biased
federal policies such as skewed GI grants. The power of exclusion
continues to be immense.

It is clear that our society will not have peace-with-justice until such shameless policies and practices are forcefully redressed. It
is important that the church leads in this urgent and difficult debate, a debate that will engage the church many of whose members
occupy the ownership class. It is for that reason that the church has
well learned to read the Bible with an exclusion of these matters
even though they are prominent in the Scriptures.

I notice that the end of the paragraph in First Samuel there is
a curious note that contradicts what has gone before:

But Saul and his son Jonathan had them (that is, sword
and spear).

Of course they did! Of course King Saul and Prince Jonathan had tools and weapons that no other Israelite had. This is because the rich and powerful are always an exception to the rule. They are always an exception about food amid famine. They were an exception about drink during prohibition. And now they are an exception about testing during the virus. That exception, nevertheless, changes nothing of the reality of society.

The only poem I know about blacksmiths is the one that you, dear reader, also likely know. In 1842 Henry Wadsworth Longfellow made the village blacksmith an admired character in the community appreciated for work and stability and reliability:

> Under a spreading chestnut-tree
> The village smithy stands . . .
> Toiling,—rejoicing,—sorrowing,
> Onward through life he goes;
> Each morning sees some task begin,
> Each evening sees it close
> Something attempted, something done,
> Has earned a night's repose.
> Thanks, thanks to thee, my worthy friend,
> For the lesson thou hast taught!
> Thus at the flaming forge of life
> Our fortunes must be wrought;
> Thus on its sounding anvil shaped
> Each burning deed and thought.[7]

No doubt Philistine blacksmiths were thanked and admired by other Philistines in the same way. No doubt the Philistines did not think much about being the ownership class and having exclusive access to tools and weapons. No doubt they did not think much about disdaining "the Hebrews" who had neither tools nor weapons. They never noticed any of that because it seem so normal—normal to have a monopoly of tools and weapons, normal to have the upper hand about food and security. They never noticed. The gospel, however, notices all of those who lack the tools and instruments essential for wellbeing, security, and prosperity. We

7. Longfellow, "The Village Blacksmith."

who are situated in the gospel are mandated to notice, even when such notice bites against our perceived vested interest; attention must be paid; redress must be imagined.

4

THE GOD OF THE SECOND WIND

WE HAVE BECOME ALL too familiar with the desperate plea, from Rodney King to George Floyd, "I can't breathe." "Breathe" is the gift of the creator God that allows us to be fully creaturely in the world. In biblical testimony, human life begins with the gift of breath:

> Then YHWH God formed man from the dust of the ground, and breathed into his nostrils the breath (*nishemah*) of life; and the man became a living being. (Gen 2:7)[1]

(The process is endlessly reiterated, as inhaling is the first thing a newborn does.) Breath belongs to God; we do not own our breath and we cannot "hold it"; but we rely on that moment-by-moment gift of God's goodness. Without that constant gift of breath, the "dust" of Gen 2:7 can only remain mere dust, and eventually it is "dust to dust." With that gift of breath from God we receive energy, freedom, power, and imagination. Having the gift of breath permits us to do the things that make us truly and fully human:

—With the gift of breath, *we can praise*:

---

1. I have taken the liberty of utilizing two Hebrew words in this exposition, *nishemah* and *ruaḥ*; the two words have different nuances but they belong to the same semantic field.

> I will praise YHWH as long as I live;
>> I will sing praise to my God all my life long. (Ps 146:2)

Some translations render "while I have breath"; in v. 4, there is mention of breath (*ruaḥ*) that departs. But until breath departs, we are able to praise. Praise is a willing act of acknowledgment of our complete reliance upon the creator who gives breath.

—With the gift of breath, *we can hope.* So in the classical tradition: "While I breathe, I hope" (*dum spiro spero*). The phrase is variously attributed to Cicero or even to St. Andrew. It is such creator-given breath that evokes passion for new historical possibility. That passion, moreover, cannot be smothered out, not even by the most vigorous, cruel effort of abuse or even slavery. For that reason every breathing human person always remains a potentially subversive agent in the world.

—With the gift of breath, *we can govern.* In the Genesis narrative Joseph, who will govern Egypt on behalf of Pharaoh, is empowered by God's breath/spirit (*ruaḥ*) for the work of governance:

> Pharaoh said to his servants, "Can we find anyone else like this—one in whom is the breath/spirit (*ruaḥ*) of God?" (Gen 41:38)

Isaiah anticipated the coming "branch" from Jesse who will govern well:

> The breath/spirit (*ruaḥ*) of YHWH shall rest on him,
>> the breath/spirit (*ruaḥ*) of wisdom and understanding,
>> the breath/spirit (*ruaḥ*) of counsel and might,
>> the breath/spirit (*ruaḥ*) of knowledge and the fear of
>> YHWH.
> His delight shall be in the fear of YHWH. (Isa 11:2–3).

Later, Isaiah awaits the servant who will be invested with the *ruaḥ* by God and who thereby is able to bring justice to the nations:

> He is my servant, whom I uphold,
>> my chosen, in whom my soul delights;
> I have put my breath/spirit (*ruaḥ*) on him;
>> he will bring forth justice to the nations (Isa 42:1)

It is all because of the breath/spirit (*ruaḥ*) of God! Such governance is in contrast to princes who lack the breath/spirit and are unable to offer "help":

> Do not put your trust in princes,
>> in mortals, in whom there is no help.
> When their breath (*ruaḥ*) departs, they return to the earth;
>> on that very day their plans perish. (Ps 146:3–4)

—With the gift of breath, *we can create*, that is, engage imagination to generate artistic beauty and splendor:

> I have filled him with divine breath/spirit (*ruaḥ*), with ability, intelligence, and knowledge in every kind of craft, to devise artistic designs, to work in gold, silver, and bronze, in cutting stones for setting and in carving wood, in every kind of craft. (Exod 31:3–4)

> He has filled him with divine breath/spirit (*ruaḥ*), with skill, intelligence, and knowledge in every kind of craft, to devise artistic designs, to work in gold, silver, and bronze, in cutting stones for setting, and in carving wood, in every kind of craft. (Exod 35:31–33)

It is why we recognize that good art work "takes our breath away"! Or as we say, "It is inspired."

The breath marks the wonder of human vitality to flourish as *praise, hope, governance,* and *artistry!* Without looking beyond this set of texts, we are able to see why it is that human persons are "little lower than God" (Ps 8:5). Even with his singularly "high" view of God, Karl Barth can say of this gift of human imagination:

> Imagination, too, belongs no less legitimately in its way to the human possibility of knowing. A man without imagination is more of an invalid than one who lacks a leg. But fortunately each of us is gifted somewhere and somehow with imagination, however starved this gift may be in some or misused by others. In principle each of us is capable of divination and poetry, or at least capable of receiving their products.[2]

---

2. Barth, *Church Dogmatics* III/1, 91.

All of this is a gift of God. There is no "breath" that is autonomous. Thus the Psalmist can readily recognize:

> When you hide your *face*, they are dismayed;
>> when you take away their breath (*ruah*), they die
>> and return to their dust.
> When you send forth your spirit (*ruah*), they are created;
>> and you renew the *face* of the ground. (Ps 104:29–30)

It is worth noting that the double use of "breath" (*ruah*) occurs in chiastic parallel to "face."

For the interpreter who desires more textual grist for the exposition of "breath," we may refer to the neglected words of Elihu in Job 32–37:

> But truly it is the spirit (*ruah)* in a mortal,
>> the breathe (*nishemah*) of the Almighty that
>> makes for understanding. (Job 32:8)

> The spirit (*ruah)* of God has made me,
>> and the breath (*nishemah*) of the Almighty gives
>> me life. (Job 33:4)

> If he should take back his spirit (*lev*) to himself,
>> and gather to himself his spirit *(ruah)* and his
>> breath (*nishemah*),
> all flesh would perish together,
>> and all mortals return to dust.
> (Job 34:14–15; author's translation)

Elihu is unambiguous; the breath on which human persons depend is wholly the gift of God! No human agent has the right to take it away! In this Elihu echoes Job's own conviction:

> In his hand is the life of every living thing (*nephesh*)
>> and the breath (*ruah*) of every human being.
> (Job 12:10)

Given this wonder of breath, we may ask how it is that one loses one's breath or becomes "short of breath." What is it that takes our breath away? I will identify of four such causes of shortness of breath, but it would be easy to think of more:

- Stunning *beauty* can take one breath away, a vista of nature, a work of art, or a piece of music. Such beauty summons us to yield ourselves to what is beyond our control or explanation.

- As we are learning, *pollution* can take our breath away. And now with the virus and the resulting industrial slow-down, we are witnessing clean air and the unexpected capacity to breathe freely that had been lost with smog.

- *Fear* can take our breath away as we may be paralyzed and frozen in the face of profound threat.

- Just now we are discovering that *violence* can take our breath away. This reality is on exhibit in the rampage of violence that is now epidemic among us, the kind of violence that has historically enjoyed social approval.

It turns out that a legacy of slavery that placed Blacks in an unbearable circumstance, perforce, legitimated the role of "slave drivers" whose plantation work was to keep slave Blacks "in their place" and productive. There is a line that can be drawn from the role of *slave drivers* to that of the historical role of *police* whose work was to protect white persons and white property from the reach of the underclass of disadvantaged Blacks. Police are caught in a web of racism not of their making with a role assigned them that tilts toward racist violence. We are now witnessing the culmination of that long-standing role of authorized violence toward those who have been accorded no legal protection and no assurance against undue violence. Those who fulfill that continuing role of enforcement have learned that the most effective way to control such persons is to deny them breath. Thus the desperate cry, "I can't breathe," is no accident; it is the intended outcome of the immobilization of those who are perceived as social threats.

And when breath is taken away, those deprived of breath lose their capacity for *praise, hope, governance, and artistry*, that is, the loss of elemental human functions. It falls to police to decide who shall breathe and who shall not, that is, who shall live and who shall not. To take breath away is to assume the role of God. So now we live in a society that is short—in fear, anger, hate, and violence—of breath. The burden of that shortness of breath falls on the most vulnerable in our society, Black people. One does not hear of the choking of even the poorest white, though it may happen and be unreported. We can readily transpose the wisdom of Proverbs from "the poor" to Blacks because both are among the most vulnerable. That wisdom asserts:

> He who mocks the poor insults their Maker. (Prov 17:5)

When anyone is deprived of breath, the God who gives breath is violated.

Now we can see the work that arises for the faithful community in such a breath-denying society. The people of God are a people of the "second wind," the recovery of breath after the loss of breath. The God who gave the first breath in Genesis is the God who gives a second wind to those who are willing and able to inhale the goodness of God that yields courage, stamina, and steadfastness.

—Thus Ezekiel can address Israel in exile with anticipation:

> Thus says the Lord YHWH to these bones: I will cause breath (*ruaḥ*) to enter you, and you shall live. I shall lay sinews on you, and will cause flesh to come upon you, and cover you with skin, and put breath (*ruaḥ*) in you, and you shall live; and you shall know that I am YHWH . . . Then he said to me, "Prophesy to the breath (*ruaḥ*), prophesy, mortal, and say to the breath (*ruaḥ*): Thus says the Lord YHWH, "Come from the four winds (*ruaḥ*), O breath (*ruaḥ*), and breathe (*nph*) upon these slain, that they may live." I prophesied as he commanded me, and they lived, and stood on their feet, a vast multitude. (Ezek 37:5–6, 9–10)

A second wind permits those denied breathe to stand up again, that is, those in exile may receive homecoming. Now it is the work of the faithful to create policies and practices, institutions and a culture in which the deprived of breath can live and stand on their feet.

—After the execution of Jesus, his disciples were hiding in despairing fear. And then, with the doors locked, he came and stood among them (John 20:19):

> He said to them again, "Peace be with you. As the Father has sent me, so I send you." When he had said this, he breathed (*enephusēsen*) on them and said to them, "Receive the Holy Spirit." (vv. 21–22)

The church in its fearful hiding, like Israel, is given a second wind. The church is sent to perform the new regime of Jesus. That new regime, surely, means the restoration of full human capacity to those long denied a first breath. It is the work of the church to relay that second wind from Jesus to those most short of breath.

—The breath of Jesus is inhaled in the book of Acts as Pentecost:

> Suddenly from heaven there came a sound like the rush of a violent wind (*pnoē*), and it filled the entire house where they were sitting (Acts 2:2)

The rest is history. The book of Acts narrates the way in which this odd community of the second wind "turned the world upside down" (Acts 17:6). It is task of this breathed-on community to do the work of turning our world of racist violence upside down. When it is turned *upside down* it will be *right side up*.

—The church of the second wind can sing in familiar, albeit somewhat romantic cadence:

> Breathe on me breath of God;
> fill me with life anew,
> that I may love what you dost love,
> and do what thou wouldst do.[3]

Less familiarly in another Pentecost hymn, the church can sing:

> Keep us fervent in our witness,
> unswayed by earth's allure,

3. *Glory to God*, 286.

Ever grant us zealous fitness,
which you alone assure
Come, come, come, Holy Spirit, come.[4]

The prophecy of Ezekiel, the breath of Jesus, the rush of the Spirit, and the *singing of the church,* all pivot on the second wind. It is time now for those who receive the new breath to relay that new capacity to breathe, to let those who have too long known, "I can't breathe." They may now with joy and freedom live out the new second wind, affirming *"I can breathe."* Those who receive the second wind are like the one healed by the apostles:

> Jumping up, he stood and began to walk . . . All the people saw him walking and praising God. (Acts 3:8–9)

4. *Glory to God,* 287.

5

THE GOD LADEN
WITH NARRATIVE SPECIFICITY
AND PARTICIPIAL CONSTANCY

IN THESE HARD DAYS every pastor (along with many other folk) is asked, "How do you fend off despair?" "How can we continue to hope?" In response to these questions, what follows here is my exposition of a single familiar text from Israel's great Manifesto of Hope, Isaiah 40–55:

> But those who wait for YHWH shall renew their strength,
>> they shall mount up with wings like eagles,
> they shall run and not be weary,
>> they shall walk and not faint. (40:31)

The statement is an adversative introduced by "but," meaning to counter the weariness, faintness, and exhaustion of v. 30. The single mandate is to "wait for YHWH." The term "wait" is in many places translated as "hope," thus "hope for YHWH." This single requirement is terse and does not by itself give us much. Until it is remembered that the name YHWH ("the Lord") is almost always inflected in the Old Testament. And when it is not inflected it is nevertheless tacitly insistent. Thus we may consider what happens when we notice the characteristic inflections of YHWH, the one in whom we are to hope.

The characteristic inflection of the name of the God of the covenant takes two forms. (Here I am indebted to the great German scholar, Claus Westermann.) On the one hand, YHWH's name is regularly embedded in narratives in which YHWH plays a decisive and specific role. Most familiarly,

> I am YHWH . . . who brought you out of the land of Egypt, out of the house of bondage. (Exod 20:1)

The formulation is more complete in Deut 8:14–16:

> . . . who brought you out of the land of Egypt,
> out of the house of bondage . . .
> who led you through the great and terrible wilderness . . .
> who made water flow for you from flint rock . . .
> who fed you in the wilderness with manna.

This narrative recital reaches its most complete articulation in Psalm 136 where we get YHWH as active subject and agent of the verbs that tell the story of Israel and of the world:

who made (v. 5)

  who spread (v. 6)

    who made (v. 7)

      who struck (v. 10)

        who brought out (v. 11)

          who divided (v. 13)

            who overthrew (v. 15)

              who led (v. 16)

                who struck down (v. 17)

                  who gave (v. 21)

This list of active, transformative verbs portrays YHWH as an active agent who creates new futures for Israel. This doxological formulation raises no questions and offers no explanations. It is simply the story that faithful Israel tells about the God for whom it waits and upon whom it hopes. Thus the single terse mandate of Isa 40:31 implies the whole range of narrative memories in which YHWH is embedded. Israel's hope is in the God who has performed all of these wonders. Israel's hope is that this God will yet again, in time to come, perform such wonders. What God has done, God will do! Hope requires knowing, treasuring, and retelling that narrative that gives inflection to the name of YHWH.

On the other hand, Israel's doxological tradition, in somewhat different grammar, makes YHWH the subject of participles that recite the characteristic actions that YHWH does over and over and continues even now. Whereas the narratives are "one-off" occasions, the participles bespeak constant actions and reliable commitments. Perhaps the most familiar and treasured such participial recital is in Psalm 103:

> . . . who forgives all your iniquity,
>> who heals all your diseases,
> who redeems your life from the Pit,
>> who crowns you with steadfast love and mercy,
> who satisfies you with good as long as you live . . . (vv. 3–5)

Here are five participles that attest YHWH's ongoing work done constantly and repeatedly. It belongs to YHWH's character to be the God who "forgives, heals, redeems, crowns, and satisfies." The God upon whom Israel waits and hopes is the God who is doing all of these things.

This doxological catalog of pastoral constancy can be readily expanded. As a show of God's power, Isaiah has it this way:

> who frustrates,
>> who makes,
>>> who turns back,
>>>> who makes,
>>>>> who confirms,
>>>>>> who fulfills,

who says,

who says,

who says,

who says (Isa 44:25–28)

The repeated use of "who says" exhibits YHWH's capacity to authorize and command by utterance. Or in the book of Job:

who gives,

who sends,

who sets,

who frustrates,

who takes,

who saves (Job 5:10–15).

who removes,

who overturns,

who shakes,

who commands,

who stretched,

who trampled,

who made,

who does great things beyond understanding,

and marvelous things without number.

(Job 9:5–10)

The participial form lends itself variously to the historical requirements of Israel, or to the majestic sweep of all creation. In both modes, in history and in creation, YHWH is affirmed as the God who gives, sustains, and governs life, and who resists the powers of death. The mood of doxology is so confident and so sweeping that in the voicing of Israel there can be no hindrance or hesitation about the wondrous capacity of YHWH.

When Isaiah bids Israel in exile to "wait for YHWH," the one for whom Israel is to wait is the God featured in the thickness of the narratives and in the vitality of the participles. The sum of such specificity and constancy is that this God is a reliable giver and sustainer of life when all else fails. It is evident then, that the work of pastoral, liturgical, and educational leadership in the church is to create *materials* (stories, songs, dramas) whereby Israel can re-perform the narrative specificities and the participial constancies in our own particular context.

For that reason, the generative work of leadership is never finished because recitals of faith are always to be reconstituted in ways that bespeak compelling contemporaneity. Such stories, songs, and dramas are in order to exhibit the irresistible force of the God who gives life to the world. Thus the great hymns of the church have always told the story of God as creator and redeemer. The materials required for such faithfulness may be bold, confident, and artistic. (This is in contrast, for example, to many so-called "praise hymns" that are mostly lazy, anemic, and cowardly; they do not claim anything for God or assert anything remarkable beyond a recital of intimacy.)

Along with the provision of good materials for such faith, leadership is also to evoke and convene many *venues*, regular and ad hoc, large and small, where the faithful may together line out the narratives and participles which this inimitable God can inhabit.

In the provision of required *materials and venues*, we should not miss that in much of the church, conservative and liberal, we have become uneasy about such characterizations of God that constitute the core of the Bible. Conservatives tend to flatten the thickness of the narrative into a package of certitudes; liberals tend to change the subject away from vigorous holiness because such a claim is an intellectual embarrassment for "the cultured despisers of religion." We may recognize, with a good heart, that for both conservatives and liberals the church's witness to God in narrative and in participle is voiced in a different dialect that does not accommodate the "low ceiling" of modernity. Not losing heart, I suspect, requires the nerve to speak in that very different dialect.

Israel is insistent that when we wait/hope in YHWH with glad hearts and full reliance on narrative specificity and participial constancy, something remarkable may happen to us. We may "renew our strength." We may recover our courage, energy, and freedom. We may slough off the inclination to despair. Israel could indeed walk close up to despair:

> My way is hidden from YHWH,
>   and my right is disregarded by my God. (Isa 40:27)

But what refuses despair is the regular glad communal recital of the reality of YHWH. Thus our practice is to mobilize our most courageous testimony to YHWH, so that we have no room or energy left with which to inhabit the sorry condition of the world around us. Thus the prophetic bid is to

wait for YHWH,

  to hope in YHWH,

    to bet on YHWH,

      to take a chance on YHWH.

Wait, hope, bet, take a chance on the God who inhabits our stories and our participles, and then to notice how strength returns to us.

This is not new strength for self-sufficiency or self-regard for self-indulgence. It is, rather, new strength that moves us to act in generative ways:

> Those who wait for YHWH shall renew their strength,
>   they shall mount up with wings like eagles,
>   they shall run and not be weary,
>   they shall walk and not faint.

The poetry intends to move us into action at three different paces, depending upon our readiness and our capacity for engagement. We may:

Soar . . . mount up with wings like eagles,

Sprint . . . run and not be weary,

Stroll . . . walk and not faint.

What a triad of paces!

Soar . . . into bold actions of restorative freedom;

Sprint . . . make a dash for restorative justice,

Stroll . . . into the quiet steady work of peace.

In meeting regularly for shared celebration of this God, we come face-to-face with this holy character who occupies a core place in our lives. When we do not meet regularly to sing and tell and dance, this defining character disappears from our imagination and so from our lives; we are left to despair amid the hopeless condition of our common life that is defined by a narrative of death and by participles of either self-regard or self-despising. The work of faith is to keep our lives focused on this dependable One in our story. This is the one who keeps the future open, who refuses the shut-down of despair, who overrides our temptation to defeat. This is the one who makes *a way out of no way*, as was wondrously done amid the waters of the exodus and the desert of the exile (see Ps 77:19; Isa 33:8–10). When this one occupies our imagination, we are empowered to boldness, risk, and freedom, kept profoundly remote from all despair. Imagine, a way out of no way! We need only walk that way. It is no wonder we take ourselves to be followers of this more excellent way. We may do well to finish with John Calvin's great hymnic affirmation:

> Our hope is in no other save in thee;
> our faith is built upon thy promise free;
> Lord, give us peace, and make us calm and sure,
> that in thy strength we evermore endure.[1]

---

1. *Glory to God*, 624.

6

THE GOD WHO FINISHES

Tenth Sunday after Pentecost

(Gen 37:1–4, 12–28; Ps 105:1–6, 16–22, 45;
1 Kgs 19:9–18; Matt 14:22–33)

IN BASKETBALL THERE IS a word used to characterize a player who cannot score. They may dribble, pass, and guard, but they cannot score. They are not able to "finish," or to "close." The good news in today's readings is that the God of the gospel can "finish." We have three case studies concerning the ways in which God "finishes," each of which echoes the great "finish" of creation (Gen 2:2) and the great "finish" of the cross (John 19:30).

The first case study concerns Joseph. In the Genesis reading we get only a beginning of the narrative, but we get the full picture in the lyric of Ps 105:16–22, also a reading for the day. The words attest a radical reversal wrought by the word of God. The land has a famine; Joseph is s slave. But that is before the great "until" of Ps 105:19. After that turn, everything is changed. It turns out that "Joseph's life matters." It matters to the daily life of the people and it matters to the big purpose of God. The slave becomes the ruler. The dearth becomes bread (Gen 42:37). The one risen to power organizes food in order to feed both the realm of Pharaoh as well

43

as his own people, Israel (Gen 47:12). God did not quit until there was a flourishing of good food and new social possibility.

In the second case study Elijah is put to flight by the death threat of Queen Jezebel. He flees and hides out. He has been a bold advocate for the purpose of YHWH that collided with the royal a regime because it concerned a socio-economic revolution.[1] In his moment of fear, flight, and acute sense of lonely abandonment, Elijah is addressed by the God who does not quit. He is assured, against his own judgment, that he is not left as the only faithful one:

> Yet I will leave seven thousand in Israel, all the knees that have not bowed to Baal, and every mouth that has not kissed him. (1 Kgs 19:18)

YHWH has resources that continue. God had mobilized many bold witnesses who continue to keep faith and live toward the alternative world of YHWH.

The gospel reading is a third rendering of the same drama. After the hunger in of Egypt and after the threat of the National Security State of Jezebel, the third crisis is the chaos of the storm. This "battering wind" is no mere tempest on the Sea of Galilee. The storm, rather, is the raging of the chaotic waters that seek to overwhelm God's ordered creation, a forceful chaos not unlike that at the outset before God did the magisterial creative work of life-giving order (Gen 1:1–2).

As Joseph responded to the hunger in Egypt and Elijah (plus 7000!) responded to the predatory threat of Jezebel, so now against the wind of chaos, there is the dominical sway of Jesus who restrains the storm. Jesus commands "the wind to cease," the wind of life-taking disorder. This is no act of magic. It is no quieting of a small squall. It is the taming of cosmic disorder. So that we do not miss the point, Matthew in 14:33 adds a confessional affirmation that is lacking in the parallels in Mark and John. The concluding verse offered by Matthew is in order that we may understand the *depth of the storm of chaos* and *the scope of the lordly claim made*

---

1. See Brueggemann, *Testimony to Otherwise.*

44

for Jesus. In that moment of the restarting of creation the fearful disciples had a glimpse of who Jesus is. He is the creator God! He is named "Son of God," affirming an inchoate Trinitarian affirmation, because it is he who boldly manages the wind (spirit)! They recognized him for who he is; they worshipped him!

Thus the preacher's good word concerns this God who can finish with good outcomes, who is; "able to accomplish abundantly far more than all we can ask or imagine":

—Joseph gives bread.

—Elijah with remarkable force gives witness to an alternative economy.

—Jesus re-starts creation.

God has a steadfast resolve for the world:

—that food should be abundant . . . and for all;

—that the economy be recalibrated, ala Elijah and Elisha, to work justice for the left behind;

—that the world should be ordered peaceably.

That is a signature triad for the God of the gospel:

—abundant food,

—economic justice, and

—peace.

The corollary for the preacher is that this steadfast resolve of God for the world, in these three cases, is accomplished in and through human agents mobilized by God. Food is guaranteed by the organizational genius of Joseph (albeit a confiscatory genius). Economic justice is wrought through the inscrutable initiatives of Elijah and Elisha; peace is enacted by the dominical authority of Jesus. Jesus is, as Matthew attests in his own idiom, the "word become flesh." But he is flesh! He is a human actor who stands in the train of those human witnesses and agents who performed God's relentless resolve.

This second accent on human agency permits the interpreter to focus closely on Peter in the gospel reading. The storm of chaos, not surprisingly, frightened Peter. His fear, however, is effectively countered by the word of Jesus that is cast according to Israel's recurring "salvation oracles" (see Isa 43:1, 5). In that utterance the speaker declares his presence amid the chaos; by his presence he counters fear by assurance. Thus the assurance of Jesus in Matt 14:27 is a game-changer. It is a summons to Peer to move beyond and in spite of his fear to accept his human agency in God's intent.

Peter answers with a readiness to trust the word of Jesus. And then in v. 29, Jesus issues his imperative to Peter, "Come." "Come, defy the chaos. Come, trust the will of the creator for a peaceable order. Come, take a risk according to God's intent. Peter instantly, obeys . . . for an instant. But then he looks away from Jesus and see the storm. His attention is diverted from his trust in Jesus and he falls into fearfulness . . . and sinks. Thus it is for Peter a contest between *trust in the word and person of Jesus* and *fear because of the immense force of disorder.* Even in his great fearfulness, however, Peter knows to trust Jesus enough to cry out to him; and he is rescued! For good reason Jesus labels Peter as "you of little faith," a label Matthew has Jesus reiterate frequently (8:26; 16:6; 17:20).

But the wind does cease, their little faith notwithstanding! And they worshipped! They know him to be "the Son of God" who in his dominical authority reorders creation and keeps safe. Jesus as Lord of creation will be celebrated in the later epistle as the one in whom "all things hold together" (Col 1:16). The disciples had already discerned this truth of Jesus!

We are mindful that Peter is a stand-in for all of the disciples who are "of little faith," but who are also like Peter in their worship of Jesus. They are "of little faith" because following Jesus is risky business. More than that, Peter is a stand-in for the church that is to come, the church that is also summoned to risky faith and most often is of "little faith."

These readings suggest *the deep resolve of God* enacted by *human agents in ready obedience.* So now the summons to Joseph, Elijah, and Jesus becomes a summons to Peter, the disciples whom he leads, and to the church that he anticipates. These readings addressed now to the church invite the faithful to walk out over the chaos that assaults the order of God's creation. At the moment the face of that chaos is racism and white supremacy. (The face of chaos will change, but the threat remains the same.) Into that chaos now faced as racism, the Lord of the church bids us "come." He identifies us as "of little faith." And we complete the narrative by worshipping him. We worship him "in spirit and in truth" when we run the risks that are required for the recovery of a world of food, justice, and peace.

It is easy to take our eyes off Jesus and conclude that the threat of chaos (now racism and white supremacy) is beyond our capacity. The narrative affirms, to the contrary, that Peter did not need to sink. He needed only to trust Jesus, that is, to "trust and obey." When we do that, the Son of God may yet again declare, "It is finished" (John 19:30). Our prayer for the finish of God's new creation is not a passive wait. It is rather a lively engagement with and for the new possibility of food, justice, and peace:

> *Finish then thy new creation;*
>> pure and spotless let us be;
> Let us see thy great salvation
>> perfectly restored in thee:
> Changed from glory into glory,
>> till in heaven we take our place,
> Till we cast our crowns before thee,
>> lost in wonder, love, and praise.[2]

---

2. *Glory to God*, 366.

7

THE MANDATE TO BE
UNLIKE THE OTHERS

ANCIENT ISRAELITES STRUGGLED, AS do we, with public leadership. They feared, as do we, both anarchy and authoritarianism. They figured a king would curb anarchy:

> In those days there was no king in Israel; all the people did what was right in their own eyes. (Judg 17:6; 21:25)

They had an itch for kingship; but the models for kingship from surrounding states were not reassuring. Old Samuel warned them about the greedy avarice of kings:

> This will be the ways of the king who will reign over you; he will *take* your sons and appoint them to be his chariots and to be his horsemen, and to run before his chariots and he will appoint for himself commanders of thousands and commanders of fifties, and some to plow his ground and to reap his harvest, and to make his instruments of war and the equipment of his chariots. He will *take* your daughters to be perfumers and cooks and bakers. He will *take* the best of your fields and vineyards and olive orchards, and give them to his courtiers. He will *take* one-tenth of your grain and of your vineyards

and give it to his officers and his courtiers . . . (1 Sam 8:11–17)

The king will be a taker!

The tradition reports that Israel had two early failed attempts at kingship. Gideon, the great warrior, nicely refused kingship:

> I will not rule over you and my son will not rule over you;
> YHWH will rule over you. (Judg 8:23)

Gideon nonetheless practiced greed and confiscated the gold jewelry of his people (8:24–26). He turned out to be a taker just as Samuel would later warn Israel. After Gideon, Abimelech made himself king. He, however, is condemned in the narrative because he came to power only through a blood bath as he killed his seventy brothers in order to seize power (Judg 9:1–6). It was a massacre that would haunt and trouble Israel. He too was a ruthless "taker." In the end, Samuel gave in; against his better judgment and at the exhausted behest of YHWH, he anointed a king (1 Sam 8:22).

It is remarkable that Moses and the scribes included only one provision in the entire Torah concerning public leadership, that is, concerning the establishment of monarchy that would shape Israel for a long time to come (Deut 17:14–20). The covenantal tradition of Sinai is fiercely disrupted by the royal ideology of Jerusalem that would come to dominate the tradition. In response to that royal ideology and the policies and practices that it would surely generated, Moses issued a sharp and discerning warning through this single Torah provision. Moses knew that kings are inherently takers, as Israel came to know. In the end, Israel gets a king. They wanted a king to be "*like* the other nations" (1 Sam 8:5, 20), that is, equipped to "take," and to transfer wealth from subsistence peasants to the surplus of urban elites. Moses, however, intends that the king he authorizes in Israel would be *unlike* other kings. Moses specifies that *unlikeness* in three ways.

1. The king in Israel must be from "your own community" (v. 15). The Hebrew has "one from among your brothers," that is, the king shall be grounded in covenantal faith and committed to the practice of covenantal solidarity. Israel must not have a king who is

tilted toward any other ideology that is inimical to the covenantal solidarity of all of the neighbors.

2. The king in Israel is not to specialize in acquisitiveness in order to advance the king's own interest. Moses knows about the habitual cravings of powerful people. He prohibits three such seductions:

— No accumulation of horses, that is, armaments. Moses knows that an accumulation of arms can serve to enhance macho self-regard, and can readily destabilize of the nation and its neighbors.

— No accumulation of wives. The accumulation of royal wives was a strategy for building alliances and networks of power in the interest of self-securing. And even in more "modern" form, sexual acquisitiveness is an exercise in macho assertion that leads to socio-economic exploitation.

— No accumulation of silver and gold, no exploitation of royal power for the sake of self-enrichment. For that very reason we have in the US a clause against emolument; even if the clause is poorly enforced, it is a recognition of the usurpatious capacity of those with power.

No imagination at all is required to see that this triad of prohibitions is aimed in quite specific ways at the avarice of King Solomon, the model of an acquisitive king.[1] It is reported that Solomon managed to accumulate many *horses* (and chariots) (1 Kgs 4:26), many *wives* (1 Kgs 11:1–3), and great quantifies of *silver and gold* (1 Kgs 10:14–25). It is evident that Solomon was not grounded in covenantal faith; he lived and ruled as if he were not "from the community," not a brother in covenant. In the same way it takes no imagination to see that even in a contemporary political economy with an emolument clause, the same triad of acquisitiveness is ready at hand. Such accumulation, ancient or contemporary, decisively alters the vision actions of those in power. These practices of accumulation will cause, says Moses, a "return to Egypt" (Deut

1. See Brueggemann, *Solomon*, 139–59.

17:16; see the ultimate covenantal curse of Deut 28:68). The phrase does not concern any geographical relocation. Rather it bespeaks an adoption of Pharaoh-like policies and practices that will reduce vulnerable subjects to something like slavery, or at least to abject poverty and hopeless debt.

3. A king who does not engage in acquisitiveness has time on his hands. Moses proposes that with that free time, the king has opportunity for a very different exercise, namely, reading the Torah. The term rendered "copy" in 17:18 is in Greek *deuteros* (= second) and in context likely refers to some form of the book of Deuteronomy that is a "second version" of the Torah through which the ancient covenant of Sinai was reinterpreted to guide Israel in the new context of the land. The king is to study the book of Deuteronomy! What the king will find as he studies the book of Deuteronomy is that the Lord of the Torah has a pronounced inclination toward the left behind . . . widows, orphans, and immigrants (Deut 10:18; 14:29; 16:11, 14; 24:17, 19). The primary accent of the Torah of Deuteronomy is that the community must pursue "justice and only justice" (16:20), by which is meant restorative justice for the economically disadvantaged. For good reason, a cornerstone of Deuteronomy is the provision for the "year of release" (15:1–18) whereby debts are cancelled so that indebted poor people can reenter the economy in a viable way.

We may notice, moreover, that the Torah provision for kingship (Deut 17:14–20), is situated in the book of Deuteronomy along with other identifiable "public offices" including judges (17:8–13), priests (18:1–8), and prophets (19:15–22). Thus the king is a part of a larger system of governance and is not free to be authoritarian or arbitrary in power. Norbert Lohfink has suggested that this set of texts is an early proposal for "the separation of powers."[2] Dean Mc-Bride has gone further to propose that the book of Deuteronomy is a "constitution" for the governance of ancient Israel.[3] Thus the book of Deuteronomy, given by Moses and the scribes, situates the role of the king in a larger and carefully arranged grid of authority

2. Lohfink, *Great Themes from the Old Testament.*
3. McBride, "Polity of the Covenant People," 233–34.

and responsibility, all of which is to curb avarice in the royal office and to define royal authority in terms of the Sinai covenant that is preoccupied with care for the neighbor and the neighborhood.

There is of course no straight line from this ancient text to our present world, and in any case the US isn't a theocracy, at least not yet! Nevertheless we are able to see in this text an early effort at something like a covenantal-democratic notion of governance that makes a key commitment to the neighborhood. In broad outline it is possible to trace the public trajectory from the old Sinai tradition through the tradition of John Calvin that eventuated, among other things, in the social vision of the Puritans in the United States.

This scenario of governance invites women and men of faith to consider public office, and specifically the office of the president in terms of this old tradition. We might even suggest that this text from Moses provides some workable criteria for thinking faithfully about the election:

—the difference covenantal grounding might make;

—the importance of a decisive check on self-serving acquisitiveness;

—the crucial commitment to a neighborly Torah.

If we can make appeal to the "exceptionalism" of the US (as the slogan, "Make America Great Again" surely means to do), we might expect that the office of president should be exceptional, unlike any other form of power. But alas, we can clearly see now the failure of the "separation of powers" of the constitution now largely collapsed into presidential authority . . . or whim. But this notion of exceptional neighborly governance is unmistakably deeply rooted in biblical faith. It is a vision of governance that was sung about in the Jerusalem temple:

> Give the king your justice, O God,
>   and your righteousness to the king's son.
> May he judge your people with righteousness,
>   and your poor with justice.
>   . . .

may he defend the cause of the poor of the people,
give deliverance to the needy,
    and crush the oppressor . . .
For he delivers the needy when they call,
    the poor and those who have no helper.
He has pity on the weak and the needy,
    and saves the life of the needy.
From oppression and violence he redeems their life;
    and precious is their blood in his sight.
    (Ps 72:1–4, 12–14)

There must be high irony in the fact that this psalm (plus only one other!) has a superscription linking it to Solomon. The acquisitiveness of Solomon characterized in the biblical text is in every way the very antithesis of this psalm in its focus on social justice. The psalm affirms that the prosperity and wellbeing of Israel depend upon such social vision, social policy, and social practice. For that reason, justice and righteousness for the poor and disadvantaged is at the center of leadership. The sad alternative to such vision, policy, and practice is a "return to Egypt," that is, a reemergence of the life-shattering oppression of Pharaoh. The Torah provision of Deut 17:14–20 and the lyrical invitation of Psalm 72 give us no straight line to our contemporary political decision-making. They do, nevertheless, lay out a trajectory of faithful thinking and acting in the public domain that will lead to common wellbeing. They constitute a summons to a different engagement in public reality.

8

THE PROTOCOLS OF SCARCITY

IN SEVERAL OF MY previous comments I have referred to "the protocols of scarcity." In this setting I want to exposit what I mean by
that phrase. "Protocols" are rules of procedure for the accomplishment of a specific task. They may be official rules that are spelled
out; but often they are tacit conventions to which everyone sub-
scribes without awareness. They are simply the accepted way of
proper procedure for given tasks to which we all agree.

When I refer to "protocols of scarcity" I am not thinking of
official rules. I have in mind, rather, the tacit conventional assumptions by which the economy tends to operate in our society. The
phrase is intentionally ambiguous. On the one hand, it may specify
the best way to proceed in the economy in which we face the given
reality of scarcity. This would be the intent of Milton Friedman, the
great apostle of scarcity, who could readily assert that economics is
"the study of the distribution of scarce resources." That is, scarcity
is a given reality and we must cope with it in a proper, responsible
way. On the other hand, however, the phrase can also mean that
there are procedures to be followed in order to create, maintain,
and manage economic scarcity. The rules are important; if they are
violated then we might not face scarcity. Thus a more conventional

assumption affirms that such "protocols of scarcity" are mandated by reality.

But in a more suspicious perspective (that I intend) the protocols function to maintain and legitimate a certain claim that is "socially constructed." My exposition, based in this suspicion, intends to challenge the first understanding that is widely assumed among us. That is, scarcity is a "social fact" created to serve certain identifiable interests. On that basis I could identify four "rules" of procedure that are widely accepted that serve to champion and maintain an economy of scarcity.

1. **Pay the lowest wages possible**. Current conversation concerning the "minimum wage" is a recognition that low pay for workers will continue to be a measure of the wellbeing or failure in society. The "rule" of low pay is an indication that the ownership-managerial class intends to keep all that it can for itself and pay only enough to workers to assure a reliable dependable work force, but not enough to provide workers with a viable life. Thus the ownership class is "unable" to pay more. The sustained effort to destroy labor unions and enact so-called "right to work" laws is an attempt s to minimize the bargaining power of labor so that labor is at the mercy of the management class. A fair wage is at the center of biblical faith in its concern for a viable society. Indeed the beginning story of the Bible in Pharaoh's Egypt and the ominous threat of "return to Egypt" put the matter of fair wages at the center of the narrative.

We may notice two references that concern exactly equitable wage practices. In the Torah of Moses, this is the requirement:

> You shall not withhold the wages of poor and needy laborers, whether other Israelites or aliens who reside in your land in one of your towns. You shall pay them their wages daily before sunset, because they are poor and their livelihood depends on them. (Deut 24:14–15)

The Torah knows about wage theft and delayed payment. Moses forbids saying to a worker, "The check is in the mail." And in Jeremiah 22 the prophet notices that King Jehoiakim brings "woe" upon himself by his maltreatment of his workers:

> Woe to him who builds his house by unrighteousness,
>   his upper rooms by injustice;
> who makes his neighbors work for nothing,
>   and does not give them their wages. (Jer 22:13)

The prophet asserts that laborers are "neighbors" who are entitled to justice. Biblical faith, "in the law and in the prophets" speaks against the exploitation of workers. The parable of Jesus in Matt 20:1–16, moreover, takes up wage payment as a metaphor for the coming kingdom. The intent of the parable is, of course, not confined to this horizon; but the verdict of the landowner in the parable requires thinking beyond narrow transactional economics:

> Friend, I am doing you no wrong; did you not agree with me for usual daily wage? Take what belongs to you and go; I choose to give to this last the same as I give to you. Am I not allowed to do what I choose with what belongs to me? Or are you envious because I am generous?" So the last will be first, and the first will be last. (Matt 20:13–15)

2. **Charge high interest on loans**. As interest rates rise for many of us, we are aware that there continues to be legal permission for exploitative pay-day loans to take advantage of the most vulnerable. Indeed the more vulnerable and dependent a borrower is, the more likely the interest rate is sure to be predatory in a way that precludes viable repayments of the loan. Again the Torah of Moses is alert to the ordinary rules of exploitation and asserts a firm limit against such a rule:

> You shall not charge interest on loans to another Israelite, interest on money, interest on provisions, interest on anything that is lent. On loans to a foreigner you may charge interest, but on loans to another Israelite you may not charge interest, so that YHWH your God may bless you in all your undertakings in the land that you are about to enter and possess. (Deut 23:19–20)

This provision limits exploitation to "foreigners." But the provision for interest-free loans to Israelites shows an awareness that interest on loans is destabilizing for a community. The readiness of the New Testament to include Gentiles in the covenant would suggest that the prohibition of interest on loans to insiders might now include the *newly welcomed insiders* who are also protected from exploitation.

The teaching of Moses is a radical rejection of our usual political economy. High interest rates suggest and assume that money is hard to come by and in its scarcity one may expect to pay dearly for it. Milton Friedman's endless mantra is, "Tighten the money supply." The expectation of the Bible, against such costliness is the insistence that the resources of the community must be generously shared without exploitative conditions with every member of the community.

3. **Practice regressive taxation**. It is not a secret that in recent time federal tax policy has become increasingly regressive. The "tax cut" of 2017 gave "relief" to the most wealthy at the expense of lower income wage earners. When an oligarchy of wealth controls the government and its tax policy as is now the case in our economy, the tax burden is predictably shifted to those who are left out of the decision-making process.

We have one remarkable narrative in the Bible about a tax crisis. When Rehoboam succeeded his father Solomon on the throne in Jerusalem, he was surrounded by young advisors who, in their lack of wisdom or experience, urged the new king to establish "a new world order" of heavy taxation to be paid by ordinary workers. In 1 Kings 12, the older, wiser, more experienced advisors urged restraint and moderation on the young king. But the young hot-shot advisors knew better; the king disregarded restraint and proceeded without regard to social risk with higher taxes. His young advisors urged on him defiance and cynicism in an ancient version of "Let them eat cake":

> My little finger is thicker that my father's loins [sic!] Now, whereas my father laid on you a heavy yoke, I will add to your yoke. My father disciplined you with whips, but I will discipline you with scorpions. (vv. 10–11)

The results of this tax policy were of course disastrous for the king and his company, as the northern state of Israel seceded from the regime in Jerusalem. As is always the case, the proponents of such regression lived in a bubble of privilege without any awareness of the reality of the working class. This practice of scarcity led to disaster because it operated in a pretend world of ignorance and greed.

4. **Keep vulnerable people debt-dependent**. What appear to be generous credit arrangements serve to seduce vulnerable people into irresponsible debt. The result of unmanageable debt is that the burden of interest payments prevents ever paying off the loan. When vulnerable people can be trapped in such debt they become dependent upon the creditor class and easily lose their capacity for political agency in the economy. David Graeber has shown that since the beginning of an organized economy the goal of the wealthy has been to create a debtor class that becomes in time a reliable labor force without agency.[1] Graeber observes that the endless, oft-repeated cry of revolution in every economy of debt is "burn the records," that is, the records of endless debt, because when the papers are destroyed the debt cannot be collected.

In the Old Testament the prudent wisdom teachers understood the lethal risk of debt and warned that debt must be carefully avoided:

> The rich rules over the poor,
>> and the borrower is slave of the lender. (Prov 22:7)

But the Torah provision is more poignant and sober about economic reality. It sees that many end in debt. The Torah knows that debt is everywhere and cannot be avoided. After the wise warning of debt avoidance, there must be a way of debt relief that in the Torah is spelled out as "the year of release" that subsequently became the practice of the Jubilee year. The provision for debt relief in Deut 15:1–18 is astonishing on two counts. First, Moses does aver the familiar notion that "there will always be poor [that is, indebted] people" (v. 11; see Mark 14:7). That verdict of Moses

---

1. Graeber, *Debt: The First 5,000 Years*.

however is not a statement of resignation. Rather the statement is to underscore the urgency of this provision for debt cancellation, for such action will make it possible that poverty can be eradicated (v. 4). Debt relief is necessary to prevent the emergence of a permanent poverty class. Poverty grounded in debt can be overcome! It must be overcome for the sake of the covenant of neighbors.

Second, this text contains five usages of the *absolute infinitive*, more uses than in any other biblical text. The absolute infinitive is a grammatical device in Hebrew that cannot be spotted in English translation. It repeats the verb a second time in order to intensify the verb as an imperative. The five uses suggest the urgency of this provision for debt cancellation, the command concerning debts about which the tradition is most insistent of all commands. The five uses are:

Only obey (v. 5)

Rather open (v. 8)

Willingly lend (v. 8)

Open (v. 11)

Provide liberally (v. 14).

In Hebrew, each of these uses reiterates the verb for emphasis. This must be done! Nothing can be more important for the covenant than the cancellation of debt! The theme is echoed in the Lord's Prayer wherein we pray regularly for the forgiveness of debt (Matt 6:12). Sharon Ringe has shown how the prayer stands in the tradition of debt cancellation and the practice of Jubilee.[2] It is comforting to us in the ownership class that we have conventionally siphoned off the prophetic dimension of prayer by translating it more easily as "trespasses" or "sins." The Bible resists the legitimacy of long-term debt that keeps the vulnerable in thrall in a way that skews both the economy and the neighborhood.

It is easy to see that on all these counts the good news of the Bible is a rejection of the protocols of scarcity. Against these widely

---

2. Ringe, *Jesus, Liberation, and the Biblical Jubilee.*

and conveniently held notions of scarcity, the Bible insists upon beginning with the abundance willed by the creator God. This insight that the Bible resists the protocols of scarcity presents an urgent mandate to the church and its preachers. The first work of the church is to expose the force of scarcity that is imposed by fear that is readily exploitative. Beyond expose, it is the work of the church to assert an alternative way in the world, a way of generosity that permits economic justice inclusive of every member of the community, that is, all of the neighbors. In his summary relayed to John about his ministry, Jesus provided a roster of those whom he had rehabilitated: the blind, the lame, lepers, the deaf, and the dead (Luke 7:22). His final accent in this summary is that "the poor have good news." The good news that the poor receive is relief from the protocols of scarcity that turn out to be false and enslaving. Such witness against those protocols is not incidental to the gospel. It is the core of the news entrusted to us.

9

THE SURPRISE
OF FREE HEALTH CARE

LINGER FOR SOME TIME over these theses:

1. The creator God has ordered the world to be an *arena of teeming abundance.*

2. We have imposed *protocols of scarcity* on God's abundance, so that most human persons are denied access to the abundance of God.

3. The "Kingdom of God" is the arrival of *an economy of abundance* wherein all creatures (the blind, the lame, lepers, the poor!) have access to God's abundance, and the protocols of scarcity are nullified.

4. The church is the avant-garde community that is formed in order to *embrace and practice God's abundance,* even while the old protocols of scarcity seem to prevail.

5. Part of the church's faithful practice of God's abundance is to require that the abundance of God pertains to and is *implemented through public policy.*

The church (and its pastors) will do well to pay close steady attention to the narratives of Elisha in 2 Kings, because these narratives articulate and dramatize the economic crisis of abundance and scarcity.[1] The royal economy, presided over by King Ahab and Queen Jezebel and enjoyed by the privileged, monopolized social wealth for the sake of their urban surplus. But all around the edges of the royal economy was an alternative peasant economy that continued to practice generosity. Elisha, in these narratives, is presented as a point person and exemplar of an economy of abundance that by his remarkable transformative actions subverted the interests and effectiveness of the royal economy. It is no wonder that Elisha dazzled his contemporaries, continues to dazzle readers of his stories, and has bamboozled critical scholarship that has no categories by which to "explain" his inexplicable effectiveness as an economic player.

1 See Brueggemann, *Testimony to Otherwise.*

10

THE TASKS OF OUR FAITH IDENTITY

(Josh 24:1–3, 14–25; Ps 78:1–7;
1 Thess 4:13–18; Matt 25:1–13)

BECAUSE I WRITE THIS prior to the election of 2020, I do not know the outcome of the election. No doubt some of us will be soaringly elated and some of us will be deeply chagrined by that outcome. The pastoral task on this Sunday is to call the faithful away from either elation or chagrin back to the more elemental realities of our faith. In my church calendar, this Sunday is designated as "Stewardship Sunday" in which many congregations have their annual awkward talk about money. But money-talk in the church is simply incidental to the more elemental realities of our faith that persists in its promises and its demands regardless of election outcomes.

These lectionary readings strain to assert that this moment, right now, is a freighted moment of deep urgency for the life of the world. Thus:

— The epistle reading in 1 Thessalonians 4 awaits "the sound of the trumpet" with the inexplicable arrival of new life.

— The parable in Matthew 25 anticipates the dramatic coming of the bridegroom.

— The Joshua narrative asserts that we must "choose today."

This triad of trumpet, bridegroom, and "choose today" together suggest that this is a laden moment in the life of faith. This moment that these texts characterize as urgent is opportunity to talk about our "treasure" as way of locating the location our heart, our passion, and our deep purpose in life that runs deeper than the election. Whether the election turns out well for Biden or for Trump, we are at a new beginning in our political economy, because social reality will not wait on an election. It is the work of faith to attest that this new beginning is not simply a reiteration of old conservative mantras or of old progressive good intentions. It is rather a moment when we may consider that God is doing a new thing, so that the old things we may cherish must be relinquished. The "old things" to be relinquished are not incidental or private pet projects, but whatever it is that resists the purpose of God for our life in the world. The "new thing" to be received is not a proposal by Biden or Trump, but a newness of what God wills for the world. It is possible, I suggest, to see three dimensions of this kairotic urgency that may be the grist of our preaching.

First, our work is to *recover the alternative narrative of faith.* Psalm 78, the Psalm for the day, invites Israel to "tell the coming generation" about its memory of God's goodness, so that they can "set their hope in God" and "keep his commandments" (v. 7). This narrative of God's goodness is alternative to the dominant narrative of self-sufficiency into which Israel had been seduced. We will not transmit the alternative of faith to our children until and unless we identify that dominant narrative into which we have been seduced. The dominant narrative among us is one of US exceptionalism that makes our culture privileged, entitled, and righteous. It is a story of white domination that received its wealth as a result of providential generosity. It is a story of male domination in which history is made by noble white men.

The alternative US story to be recovered in the wake of the election as the US story is a story of greedy violence that took Native American land by genocide and that depended upon Black slaves to generate wealth. But it is at the same time also a story in which all persons "are created equal, a claim advanced by the likes of Abraham Lincoln and Lyndon Johnson, and now in the wake of the election, an alternative awaiting actualization. It will be a story not grounded in fear, greed, and violence, but a story that pivots on the generosity, civility, and restorative justice that honors all the neighbors (all Black and Hispanic and Asian neighbors), that protects all gay and lesbian neighbors, and that provides for all poor and needy neighbors.

This alternative story is deeply grounded in the gospel. But it is not only a gift. It is an assignment. It is a task to be done in the intimate places where we tell our treasured stories, in the marketplaces where we bargain and trade, and in public places where we make policies concerning debt and taxes. This is a time to get our story straight, to engage that narrative that we have nearly forfeited in our narcoticized indifference. Our children will thank us for that work.

Second, our work is to *put away foreign gods*. The drama of the Joshua text has this imperative as the primary requirement for covenant with YHWH. In the ancient world "foreign gods" were actual material icons of which archaeologists have found so many. Already in Gen 35:1–4 it is reported that Jacob required his household to "put away foreign gods," and he hid them (ear rings and all!) under an oak tree, taking them out of commission. Our "foreign gods" are not so readily "handled" as that, as they are more likely ideas and ideologies that have compelling force among us. Thus a congregation might spend some energy identifying foreign gods that operate with authority to distort our lives and talk us out of our true selves. No doubt our "foreign gods, causing us to be alienated from our faith and our true selves, include racism, sexism, classism, ageism, consumerism, all of the images of self that distort those who are not like us. And surely the strongest and most dangerous of those among us just now is racism. And if these foreign gods diminish the "other" who is unlike us, then "putting them away" might entail the painful process of being face-to-face with the "other" in order listen to and honor the "other" as a carrier of pain and hope that is not very different from our own pain and hope. It is not likely that we can effectively do that hard work in homogeneous communities, but must find ways to face the other physically as a compelling presence to us.

In the Joshua drama, the positive summons is to serve YHWH with completeness and reliability (24:14); this is the antithesis of "foreign gods." That imperative concerning foreign gods is up front for Joshua. And then, after a long dialogic exchange, Joshua at the end reiterates, "'then put away foreign gods and incline your hearts to YHWH, the God of Israel'" (24:23). Perhaps the entry point into this topic is to ask about the tilt of one's heart. We might pursue a riff on the "tilt of our hearts":

> But incline your hearts to him, to walk in all his ways, and to keep his commandments, his statutes, and his ordinances, which he commanded our ancestors. (1 Kgs 8:58)

In the Psalm the talk of the tilt of the heart is voiced in prayer that God should give my heart a tilt:

> Turn my heart to your decrees,
> and not to selfish gain. (Ps 119:36)

Israel is sure and has no doubt that a heart tilted toward YHWH and YHWH's commandments is the way to wellbeing. The foreign gods, however, have great force in turning our hearts away from this glad obedience. This either/or of good or bad tilt suggests to me an allusion to Paul's contrast between the desires of the flesh (Gal 5:16–21) and "the fruit of the spirit" (Gal 5:22–23). A review of Paul's two categories will help us identify the toxic force of foreign gods that talk us out of our true selves. In the end talk of "foreign gods" is not an abstract matter, but issues in real-life conduct and attitude. The foreign gods characteristically place the self in all its self-serving at the center of reality. By contrast the God of the covenant binds us in covenantal loyalty to those around us who depend on us for wellbeing. Once the foreign gods had been expelled, Joshua could make a covenant that reconfigured the lives of those present to the meeting.

The third task of the church as it returns to basics is to *watch for and receive the newness that God is working in the world*. In the Joshua text, the newness is covenant that redefined social relationships among the neighbors (Josh 24:25). It is worth noting the radicality of the covenant that moved social interaction away from calculating transactionalism to neighborly engagement with each other. This way of social relationships is variously articulated by Paul as "look to the interests of others" (Phil 2:4), or to "weep with those who weep, rejoice with those who rejoice" (Rom 12:15). Imagine rejoicing with a person of color or weeping with a Palestinian. The dramatic act of covenant-making creates a novum in the world, a newness of which the foreign gods are quite incapable.

In the New Testament texts that radical newness is voiced in figurative language. In the parable of Matthew, the imagery is of a wedding and a wedding banquet. The subtext, however, is the coming rule of God that Jesus has initiated. The work of Jesus is to initiate a new set of social possibilities that is enunciated in both his talk and in his action. For that reason the parable ends with an imperative to "keep alert" and be on notice, because the new world erupts here and there without warning. It is the work of the faithful to watch and to notice, to identify and to celebrate wherever it is that new neighborly actions are committed that make all things new. The imagery of the epistle is not easy for us; however we may take the seemingly "mythic" language of the epistle, it is testimony to the new rule of Christ and the consequent resurrection of the dead. Imagine, those dead made alive (see Luke 15:24)!

It is the work of pastoral teaching and proclamation to take these various moments of newness in the text, cast in rhetoric alien to us, and let them point to the emerging newness now in God's world. We are, as these texts attest, at a breaking moment in the life of the world. There is no going back. There is no holding on to what was. There is no chance to continue to treasure what we have long treasured that is in contradiction to the purpose of God. It is not "liberal" or "progressive" to see that the future will be a society in which all persons will share in the elemental viability of the economy. The onerous old divisions between rich and poor, male and female, white and colored, gay and straight are no longer sustainable. Such an awareness is not at all "progressive," it is *evangelical*; it is the good news:

—Joshua initiated a break with all old patterns of social interaction by binding Israel to the neighborly Torah.

—The parable urges us not to miss the new celebrative work of the bridegroom because we are ill-prepared or asleep.

—The epistle ends with the mandate: "Encourage one another" (v. 18).

This is an odd conclusion to the paragraph. "Encourage" that we will be ready for inexplicable inauguration of new social reality. This newness is not for the faint-hearted or the fearful. We are in the midst of "all things new." That newness is a gift; it is also a task, one that can only be done when we *get our story straight* and when we *expel foreign gods*. When these preliminaries are addressed, we may be at the cusp of God's new coming rule among us that will entail both cost and joy.

11

"TO HELL WITH IT" . . . NOT!

WHAT FOLLOWS HERE IS a reflection concerning three public leaders. Each of them faced an immense crisis in his time of public leadership. Each of them in turn opted for his own moment of wellbeing that required, in their judgment, neglect of the future. Each of them, in turn, in substance declared of the future, "To Hell with It," choosing to care only on their present moment of wellbeing.

The first case study from the Bible concerns Hezekiah, king in Jerusalem (715–687 BCE). Hezekiah is reckoned, in biblical assessment, to be a good king, which means that he trusted in YHWH:

> He did what was right in the sight of YHWH just as his ancestor David had done. He removed the high places, broke down the pillars, and cut down the pole. He broke in pieces the bronze serpent that Moses has made . . . He trusted in YHWH the God of Israel; so there was no one like him, or among those who were before him. For he held fast to YHWH; he did not depart from following him but kept the commandments that YHWH commanded Moses. (2 Kgs 18:3–6)

He was, however, under constant duress from the Assyrian superpower to the north that wanted access to the Mediterranean Sea. The threat from Assyria was extreme and relentless (see Isa 36–37). Hezekiah, at the behest of the prophet Isaiah, trusted in YHWH in the face of the Assyrian threat (see Isa 37:16–20). At the same time, however, the king was a realistic politician. Given the geopolitical reality he faced, he spotted a chance for security and relief from Assyria. He hoped that Babylon, as a nascent power, would be a check on Assyria. (Later on Babylon would indeed displace Assyria as the great northern superpower.) Thus King Hezekiah sought to make an alliance with Babylon. In order to advance that alliance the king welcomed the Babylonian ambassadors sent by King Merodach-baladan. In order to foster confidence with his would-be ally, Hezekiah shared with the Babylonian ambassadors information about Judah's defense system, military capacity, and economic resources:

> Hezekiah welcomed them; he showed them his treasure house, the silver, the gold, the spices, the precious oil, his whole armory, all that was found in his storehouses. There was nothing in his house or in all his realm that he did not show them. (Isa 39:2)

Imagine: sharing state secrets with a foreign ambassador!

The prophet Isaiah had ready access to the king. Isaiah had a very high view of YHWH's sovereignty as well as a shrewd sense of geopolitics. On both counts the prophet confronted the king for his careless foolishness. First he interrogates the king to be sure of his footing:

> What did these men say? From where did they come to you? Hezekiah answered, "They have come to me from a far country, from Babylon." He said, "What have they seen in your house?" Hezekiah answered, "They have seen all that is in my house; there is nothing in my house that I did not show them." (Isa 39:3–4)

Isaiah of course immediately recognizes the self-destructive folly of the king's exhibit. He knows that to reveal state secrets and state resources to a potential enemy is suicidal.

For good reason the prophet then declares, as an oracle from YHWH, a disastrous future for the royal family. The oracle is from YHWH, for YHWH intends to be trusted by the king who, for that reason, must not seek such alliances. Isaiah anticipates the brutal policy of Babylon for time to come:

> Days are coming when all that is in your house, and that which your ancestors have stored up until this day, shall be carried to Babylon; nothing shall be left, says YHWH. Some of your own sons who are born to you shall be taken away; they shall be eunuchs in the palace of the king of Babylon. (Isa 39:6–7)

The king is a good careful listener to the word of the prophet. He hears that his royal treasury will be taken away. He hears that even his own sons, the royal princes, will be taken to serve in Babylon. But he also notices that that is all! The threat does not touch him personally. He grabs at this personal immunity from the threat to come. And so he responds to the prophet:

> The word of YHWH that you have spoken is good." For he thought, "There will be peace and security in my days." (Isa 39:8)

There will "be peace in our time"! This is a strange, unexpected response to the hard word from Isaiah, for the prophet anticipates a devastating future for the kingdom. The king does not seem worried about the royal treasury for which he is responsible. He is not even vexed about the humiliation of his sons. He is not worried about the future of his realm beyond his own lifetime. It is enough for him that there will be security for him in his lifetime, because it will take Babylon a very long time to be mobilized as a real time menace to Jerusalem. In effect the king says to the prophet, "To hell with the future." As we know, moreover, Babylon did come to destroy the city and its temple. Babylon seized the royal treasury (see Jer 52:17–23). Babylon did deport royal sons and heirs (see

2 Kgs 24:10–12; 25:1–7). But the king does not care about any of that, for he himself is safe: to hell with the rest of it!

Our second case study is nearly contemporary to our own time. In the late 1930s Hitler began to extend his reach from Berlin and to threaten the nation-states of Europe. The British Prime Minister, Neville Chamberlain, sought to contain the threat of German National Socialism. In a most dramatic parley (as dramatic as the exchange of Hezekiah with Isaiah (Isa 39:1–8), or Hezekiah with the Assyrian ambassador (2 Kgs 18:19–35), Chamberlain negotiated with the Germans in Munich to return to London with a peace accord. He gladly acclaimed that the agreement he had reached assured "peace in our time." Chamberlain was not a bad or careless man; he was, unfortunately, enormously naive. Except that no one had any experience with so barbaric a threat as Hitler posed. He could not have known what portended from Berlin.

It turned out that Chamberlain's "peace in our time" was a profound illusion. Very soon Hitler began his European aggression that threatened every nation-state on the continent. Chamberlain had little sense of the ominous future his Munich agreement would permit. He did not intend it so. But it turned out that his Munich agreement was a sellout that amounted to "the hell with the future." Europe was left to its fate determined by Hitler as Judah was left to its fate from Babylon. In the case of Judah, what followed from such royal indifference was eventually destruction and exile. What followed from Chamberlain was the horror of World War II, including of course the Shoah. In both cases, the trade-off of a momentary peace for a coming devastation turned out badly. Public leaders cannot succeed with such indifference about the future.

Our third case concerning Donald Trump requires little exposition. With his fierce obsessive attentiveness to the election that he has lost, he has abandoned the governing responsibility of the presidency. Beyond his own hold on the office he has effectively said, "To hell with everything else."

- To hell with the economy and those most squeezed by the essential economic shutdown.

- To hell with the growing number of victims of the pandemic.
- To hell with our democratic institutions.
- To hell with those officials who have acted with brave integrity.

In sum, Donald Trump has declared, "To hell with the future," as though this moment of his decisive election defeat were the epicenter of human history. He would surely seek "Peace in our time," except that it would be much better to have "victory in our time."

These three leaders are very different cases but they have closely paralleled outcomes:

- Hezekiah in his foolish indifference contributed to the demise and long season of ancient Israel in exile.
- Chamberlain by his well-intentioned appeasement helped set in motion the brutality of World War II.
- Donald Trump, by his obdurant self-preoccupation, has jeopardized national security and helped generate a society that is at the edge of being ungovernable.

In the pursuit of something like "peace in our time" Hezekiah, Chamberlain, and Trump have acted in abdication of responsibility and in cynical resignation concerning the future.

The company of the faithful, however, is not permitted to engage in such abdication of responsibility, nor are we allowed to settle for cynical resignation. I suggest, to the contrary, that we faithful are summoned to two tasks that refuse such surrender of the future. On the one hand, we are called to trust God's promises of a new world to be given in God's goodness:

> For I am about to create new heavens
>   and a new earth;
> the former things shall not be remembered
>   or come to mind.
> But be glad and rejoice forever
>   in what I am creating;
> For I am about to create Jerusalem as a joy,
>   and its people as a delight. (Isa 65:17–18)

In such trust we may be about the work of generating that which God has promised. That work of generating such a future, moreover, requires patience, wisdom, resolve, courage, and freedom from old ideological assumptions. On the other hand, we faithful are called to obedience to the core mandates of faith (not to the picky quibbles) that persist as love of God and love of neighbor. The mandate to love God commends that we practice holiness, that we be acutely mindful that our lives come from God and are lived back to God. The mandate to love neighbor commends that we practice justice, that we be about the public business of creating a viable neighborly economy.

Who knew that our work, in the face of abdicated responsibility and cynical resignation is to "trust and obey"? To trust the promises and to obey the mandates! It is all about "trust and obey":

> Then in fellowship sweet we will sit at his feet,
>   or we'll walk by his side in the way;
> what he says we will do, where he sends we will go;
>   never fear, only trust and obey.
> Trust and obey, for there's no other way
>   to be happy in Jesus, but to trust and obey.[1]

When we consider the historical crises faced by these three spectacular abdicators, we can see the outcome of "trust and obey" in response to their failures:

- After Hezekiah's renege and the long term dislocation of the Jerusalem establishment, faithful Israel entered into a long season of brooding that eventuated in the poetry of later Isaiah. Thus after Isaiah 39 there is a hiatus of suffering that lasted nearly two centuries. And then came Isaiah 40–55 with its buoyant poetic vision that anticipated return and restoration for Israel:

  > For you shall go out in joy,
  >   and be led back in peace;

1. *United Methodist Hymnal*, 467.

74

the mountains and the hills before you
> shall burst into song,
> and all the trees of the field shall clap their hands.
> (Isa 55:12; see 35:8–10)

The poet, after all this time, refused to say, "To hell with the future."

- After Chamberlain came the fierce horror of World War II, the general assault on Europe, and the brutality of the death camps. Amid that violent misery, however, there were those who trusted and obeyed, who in the most generative way probed new power arrangements in the world. In a short period of time, in the wake of the war the "wise men" initiated the Marshall Plan, the United Nations, and NATO. While these power arrangements were far from perfect and in some ways quite inadequate, they are harbingers of and resources for new historical possibility. These "wise men" refused to say, "To hell with the future."

- And now we are after the election defeat of Donald Trump. Yet again the company of the faithful is called to "trust and obey," to mobilize generative juices for new historical possibility. Much, of course, depends on Joe Biden; but not everything depends on Joe Biden. Much depends upon a shared public readiness to trust the promises and to live them out, and to obey the mandates of covenantal faith. The work to be done is obvious enough:

  - to protect health care for all;

  - to restore a viable human economy that runs beyond unbearable inequality and paralyzing debt;

  - to address the continuing violence of racism;

  - to manage immigration policy in a humane, welcoming way; and

  - to act in care for a life-giving environment.

We do not lack resources or technological know-how for these hard issues. What is most urgently needed is the courage to trust and the will to obey; for sure "trust and obey," "for there's no other way"! The essential response to the dismissive "To hell with the future" by Hezekiah, Chamberlain, and Trump is precisely the word of Moses:

> Nor with our ancestors did YHWH make this covenant,
> but with us, who are all of us here alive today. (Deut 5:3)

Or the word of Mordecai to Esther:

> Who knows? Perhaps you have come to royal dignity for
> just such a time as this. (Est 4:14)

Or the word of Jesus to his disciples:

> Keep awake therefore, for you know neither the day nor
> the hour. (Matt 25:13)

We now know what happens when we have a leader who does not trust the big promises and who does not obey the core mandates. It is time now, by a mobilization of citizen power, to learn again what can happen when promises are trusted and mandates are obeyed.

12

TRUTH OR CONSEQUENCES

WHILE WE DID NOT choose it, we now live in a world evoked in large part by Donald Trump, a world of so-called "fake news" and so-called "alternative facts." It is a world already recognized by Isaiah:

> Woe to you who call evil good
>   and good evil,
> who put darkness for light
>   and light for darkness,
> who put bitter for sweet
>   and sweet for bitter! (Isa 5:20)

Jeremiah observes the same a century later:

> Search [the] squares and see
>   if you can find one person who acts justly
> and seeks the truth—
>   so that I may pardon Jerusalem.
> Although they say, "As YHWH lives,"
>   yet they swear falsely.
> O YHWH, do your eyes not look for truth? (Jer 5:1–3)

In that world matters are misrepresented, called by their wrong names or concealed in misleading euphemisms. Given that social reality, I have been thinking about truth, the way in which the gospel proclaims the truth, and the way in which the church is empowered to be a practitioner of truth. That thinking has led me to ponder three texts in particular, though you may think of many others as well.

The first text I thought of is the ninth commandment:

> You shall not bear false witness against your neighbor.
> (Exod 20:16; Deut 5:20)

The language of the commandment pertains to an oath in court. Under oath you shall tell the truth. The commandment believes that the truth can be told, a conviction clearly reflected in our familiar court oath, "the truth, the whole truth, and nothing but the truth." A trial most often consists in competing truth claims borne by different contradictory witnesses; the judge or jury must decide the truth of the case by determining which witness is a truth-teller. The truth is a faithful remembering of what happened, depending upon reliable witnesses.

Two matters merit attention. First, the prohibition concerns "the neighbor." The matter of truth-telling in court, as with all of the commandments, concerns the neighborhood; the "other" in the court case is a neighbor. Truth-telling is designed to enhance the neighborhood. Falseness diminishes the neighborhood. The truth depends upon regard for the neighbor. Second, in his exquisite exposition of the commandment Patrick Miller suggests that the eighth commandment on stealing and the ninth commandment are closely linked, that is, stealing and lying go together.[1] Lying in court has a violent effect on one's neighbor. Miller compellingly cites two cases (among others). In 1 Kings 21, Ahab and Jezebel are able to seize (steal!) the property of Naboth by lying against him:

> The two scoundrels came and sat opposite him; and the scoundrels brought a charge against Naboth, in the presence of the people. (1 Kgs 21:13)

---

1. Miller, *The Ten Commandments*, 343–86.

On the basis of their false testimony, Naboth was executed so that his property fell to the crown.[2] In Acts 5 Ananias and Sapphira withheld property from the church and lied about it. They are convicted by Peter:

> Why has Satan filled your heart to lie to the Holy Spirit and to keep back part of the proceeds of the land? . . . You did not lie to us, but to God!" (Acts 5:3–4)

Lying under oath is an act of violence against a neighbor; it is most often committed by strong neighbor against a weak neighbor, so that the court may become an arena for violence against the neighbor. Truth is enhancement of the neighborhood. Truth-telling is an act of enhancing the neighborhood. Lying, conversely, diminishes the neighborhood, for it is most often an act of self-serving that puts self over-against the neighborhood.

The second text of which I am mindful is John 1:14:

> And the Word became flesh and dwelt among us, and we have seen his glory, the glory a of a father's only son, full of grace and truth.

The Fourth Gospel is fully occupied with questions of "truth," asserting that Jesus is "the way, the truth, and the life" (John 14:6). In the doxological prologue to the gospel, the full divinity of Jesus is attested; he is the "Word of God" become "flesh." Our verse witnesses to the character of the Word, thus the character of the Father, and as result to the character of the Son. The Son is marked by the "glory" of the Father's only Son. That shared character is marked by "grace and truth." Given our modern Western assumptions, that word pair is a curious one. "Grace" we get as the self-giving generosity of God. But the term "truth" is odd in this usage and does not seem to go with "grace." It is odd for us because given the impact of Descartes, we incline to treat "truth" as "fact," a reduction of the term to propositional certitude. In order to refuse such a modern reduction, we will do well to go behind "grace and truth" in the Fourth gospel to see that in the Old Testament the same word pair

---

2. See Brueggemann, *Resisting Denial, Refusing Despair*, 68–96.

regularly is used to attest covenantal fidelity. The Hebrew terms, *hesed* and *'emeth*, bespeak readiness to act faithfully according to one's covenantal commitment. Thus the word pair appears in the defining self-revelation of God:

> YHWH, YHWH,
> a God merciful and gracious,
> slow to anger,
> and abounding in *steadfast love and faithfulness*. (Exod 34:6)

In the extended affirmation of God's care for King David in Psalm 89, the word pair recurs many times:

> I declare that your *steadfast love* is forever;
>   your *faithfulness* is as firm as the heavens. (v. 2)

> Righteousness and justice are the foundation of your
>   throne;
>   *steadfast love and faithfulness* go before you. (v. 15)

> My *faithfulness and steadfast* love shall be with him. (v. 24)

> But I will not remove from him my *steadfast love,*
>   or be false to my *faithfulness.* (v. 33)

And even in the pathos-filled response of v. 49, Israel can ask:

> Lord, where is your *steadfast love* of old,
>   which by your *faithfulness* you swore to David.

Thus it is clear that the two terms in John 1:14, "grace and truth," are an echo of Israel's faith concerning God's *hesed and amunah* that we translate regularly as "*steadfast love and faithfulness.*" Jesus' embodiment of God's own life is an embodiment of steadfast love and reliability, that is, covenantal reliability. This sense of "truth" (*amunah, emeth*) is evident even on the pernicious lips of Abimelech who insisted in "good faith" (*emeth*) (Judg 8:19), as in the parable of his frightened brother, Jotham as the demand of the bramble (Judg 8:15).[3] Thus, in our verse (John 1:14), Jesus is full of

---

3. See Brueggemann, "Refusing the Bramble."

"good faith" that he performs variously for trusting needy people all around him.

In such a usage we are a very long way from Cartesian facticity that comes to us as propositional certitude. Clearly "truth" in this trajectory from the Old Testament through the Fourth Gospel is a relational term that speaks of how it is that the Son (and the Father) will to relate to the world in self-giving ways, that is, in grace-filled ways. We can see that this usage in John 1:14 is congruent with the ninth commandment, because both texts concern fidelity toward the neighbor, and a refusal to violate or abuse the neighbor. The God of the covenant will not do that, nor will the neighbors in the covenants of Israel and the gospel.

The third text I consider is the well-known trial of Jesus before Pilate, the Roman governor (John 18:33–40). Or in the ironic sense of the Fourth Gospel, the trial of the Roman Empire before Jesus. Pilate is an embodiment of fully established imperial power. He is accustomed to imperial edicts that declare reality and pass imperial judgments off as the truth. The governor, however, is bamboozled by Jesus, because Jesus does not fit imperial categories. In his silence, Jesus is not actively defiant. He does not make any defense for himself. He refuses to engage the power of the empire that has come to think of itself as the determiner of truth.

It is clear that the governor is shaken by this presence that stands before him, defenseless, having no need to give answer. In desperation, the helpless governor, representative of the helpless empire before Jesus, asks, "What is truth?" He no longer knows. But of course Jesus does not answer. He has no need to answer. He knows, moreover, that "truth" is not a package of announcements or a collection of data. It is not an accumulation of knowledge. What Jesus embodies he has no need to declare. The narrative affirms that the truth is standing right in front of the governor. The governor, however, cannot recognize the truth that is before him, because the truth fits none of the imperial categories of certitude or control. The truth before the governor fleshed in the person of Jesus, is the reality of a self-giving self who is the historical embodiment of the self-giving God who stands over against the empire. Thus Paul Lehmann can conclude:

> The point and purpose of the presence of Jesus *in the world*, and now before Pilate, are to bear witness to the truth, that is, "to make effective room for the reality of God over against the world in the great trial between God and the world."[4]

The trial in the Fourth Gospel is indeed a trial between "God and the world," the world of imperial control. The claim of the gospel is that Jesus makes "room for God in the world." And the God for whom he makes room in the world is the God who gives God's self away in love for the world, giving "his only Son" (John 3:16). The God embodied before the governor is the one who loves the neighbor and who calls us to love the neighbor. The reason the governor cannot discern the truth before him is that "neighbor" is not a workable category in the empire. That, however, is the point of the trial, to insist on the cruciality of the neighbor, and therefore the cruciality of the commandment to love the neighbor.

We have now come full circle from the ninth commandment (Exod 20:16; Deut 5:20) to the "grace and truth" of covenantal reality (John 1:14), to the truth embodied in the neighbor-valorizing person of Jesus (John 18:38). As Moses insisted that the neighbor is the measure of truth, so Jesus performs in the most complete way the truth of neighborly love. It turns out that "truth" is utterance and action that restores, emancipates, and reconciles neighbors for a viable neighborhood. What does not do that is a lie! The way to bear false witness is to violate the neighborhood.

We can now reconsider the world in which we live, a world of so-called fake news and so-called alternative facts. The fake news of the networks, most blatantly on Fox, is not false simply because it misrepresents reality. It is fake because it violates neighborliness and willfully aims to set neighbor against neighbor in competition for scarce goods. Fake news is news that distorts the reality of

---

4. Lehmann, *The Transfiguration of Politics*, 53, and quoting Rudolf Bultmann.

generative neighborliness. Alternative facts are claims that fail to take into account the reality of the neighborhood, most centrally the reality of pain and loss. Thus it is always a lie when property and wealth are preferred to the wellbeing of the neighbors. Obviously the imperial governor could not comprehend!

In the midst if this palpable world of fake news and alternative facts, the church is put down as a truth-teller. Its work is to *tell the truth* about the neighbor and about the neighbor-loving God. Its work is to *act this truth* that valorizes the neighbor in the performance of restoration, emancipation, and reconciliation. The talk of truth and the walk of truth go together. In the initiative of Moses God stakes out a core claim for truthfulness concerning historical persons. In the restorative, emancipatory work of Jesus, God decisively radicalizes and advances the claim for neighborliness. In the wake of Moses and Jesus, the church finds its truthfulness in the neighbor. It refuses to be silenced by any other truth claim, by fake news or by alternative facts. It refuses to give in to the imperial posturing of Pilate.

No special gift of discernment is required to see that fake news and alternative facts have consequences. The central consequence is the dismantlement of public institutions and public possibilities. The consequence of lying is the seeding of hostility and enmity in the body politic. In the same way, truth-telling and truth-acting also have consequences. Truth-telling funds generative political energy, confidence in public institutions, and public sustenance for "the least." In the embrace of gospel truth or imperial truth, we choose consequences. Moses saw most clearly the consequence of that decision:

> See, I have set before you today life and prosperity, death and adversity . . . Choose life so that you and your descendants may live, loving YHWH your God, obeying him and holding fast to him; for this means life to you and length of days. (Deut 30:19–20)

In light of that either/or of Moses, Jesus knows that we cannot have it both ways:

> No one can serve two masters . . . You cannot serve God
> and wealth. (Matt 6:24, Luke 16:13)

Flannery O'Connor saw matters clearly:

> You shall know the truth, and the truth will make you
> odd.[5]

The church is now summoned to embrace its oddness in the world,
odd in its truth-telling and in its truth-doing.

---

5. Long attributed to O'Connor, but evidently not in her published works.

13

TWO QUESTIONS AT DAY BREAK

(2 Kgs 5:15–27; 1 Cor 4:6–7)

Reformation Sunday[1]

THIS LITTLE CHURCH IN Corinth acted the way churches tend to act. They worshipped and gave offerings and cared for each other. But they also were people with strong opinions who competed, quarreled, tried for control, and tried to outmuscle each other.

Sometimes the tension and conflict were acute, so acute that they alarmed the Apostle Paul who had founded this congregation and continued to care for it. In his letter to this church, Paul intervenes in the tension in the congregation. His intervention consists in two questions. The first question is: "What do you have that you did not receive?" They don't answer. Paul waits. But they only become silent and lower their eyes. The right answer for Paul is: "Nothing"; we have nothing that we did not receive as a gift. Everything we have is a gift. It is all a gift. That was the great insight that led to the Reformation of the church that we celebrate on this Reformation

---

1. This is likely my last sermon.

Sunday. It was Luther's great insight that God is a generous giver of good gifts. We call it "grace." It touches every part of our lives: "All good gifts are sent from heaven above!" None of it is earned. None of it is deserved. None of it is an achievement or an accomplishment or a possession; it is all gift.

Paul's second question: "If it is all a gift (and it is!), why do you boast of it as if it were not a gift?" Again, they do not answer. But they did boast. They boasted of their wealth or their smarts or their piety. By their boasting, they tried to prevail over each other in the church. But, says Paul, there is no ground for boasting, because it is a gift. But they had forgotten it is a gift, and so they boasted.

≈

So consider what happens when we forget that life is all a gift. Back in the sixteenth century, the time of Luther and the Reformation, the church had forgotten that God's love was a gift and tried to market it. The crassest form of marketing was the claim that if one gave money to the church some dead person would be released from hell. It was all a *quid pro quo* transaction.

And now, we live in a political economy that has forgotten it is all a gift. And when we forget that life is a gift, it all becomes a transaction, a *quid pro quo*, a trade-off. In that world, the strong prevail over the weak and the wealthy over the poor who cannot compete in the rat-race. Indeed, we have arrived at a place where we might think that those who give gifts, who give themselves away, are "suckers" and "losers." And because it is all a competition, we must always ask "What is in it for me? How do I gain and benefit?" That process is a never-win proposition because in the drive to control and win and prevail and have the most, we never have enough to be safe and happy. We must always be on the make for more. And in our drive for more, we become preoccupied with the worry that somewhere some undeserving person is getting something for nothing. And that cannot be allowed, we think, because we live in a world where there are no gifts; there are only bargains and trade-offs. We may die with the most, but it does not feel like winning. So now, as in Luther's sixteenth century, we are embedded in a social system that is greedy and parsimonious and fearful. And when we live that way, it inevitably turns to violence, because we have to do whatever we have to do in order to prevail.

∼

Given that reality, given the frightening sense that we live in a world that before our very eyes is becoming unglued, this is a time for the church to take a deep breath. It is time for church members to think again. It is time for Christians to remember our baptism and to recall what it is that we have signed on for. Quite distinct from the fearful world of *quid pro quo,* we have signed on for a different world where it is all gift. We live, we confess, in the world governed by the self-giving God. So we confess concerning Jesus that "God so loved the world that God gave God's only son" in love for the world. And in giving the Son, the Father God also gave God's own self away in love for the world. God has held nothing back from the world.

So Paul's first question lingers for us: "What do you have that you did not receive?" And our answer is, "Nothing." I have nothing that I have not received as a gift of God and as a sign of God's self-giving goodness. And because that is our faith, we know as well that the *quid pro quo* world of greed, fear, and violence is a false world. It is a phony construct, and we know better than that. So we may ponder this: We are made in the image of this self-giving God who has held back nothing from the world that God loves. And because we are made in the image of this self-giving God, it is our identity and our vocation to be self-givers in the world in the same way that God is a self-giver in the world.

Just for fun I have included in our readings today a Bible story that you may not have heard before. It concerns Elisha, the great wonder-worker in the Old Testament. In this story, Naaman, a Syria general (that is, an enemy of Israel) has leprosy (something like the virus). Elisha wondrously and mysteriously heals the enemy general of his virus. The general wants to pay Elisha for the healing, because he is accustomed to pay and is able to pay. But

Elisha will not accept any pay because the healing from God is free! No co-pay for the free gift of God! It was free because the God of Israel is a generous self-giving God, even to the enemy. Elisha says to the general, go back home and be grateful. It is all a gift!

~

So I have this vision for Reformation Sunday. Imagine this: every morning God, the self-giving creator, wakes up and asks three questions of God' self:

—God's first question every morning: *What gift shall I give today?* As we know, this God gives sun and rain. This God wills that the earth should be abundant and peaceable. This God gives healing, emancipation, transformation, and new life.

—God's second question every morning: *To whom shall I give these good gifts?* God especially notices those who are in need of good gifts. Not the rich, not the secure, not the well-connected people, but those in need, those left behind, those excluded from the goodies of the earth. In the Old Testament, God notices widows and orphans and immigrants. In the New Testament Jesus notices publicans and sinners, the blind, the lame, the deaf, the poor, the lepers (see Luke 7:22). And now in our world God notices the left behind, the poor, many people of color, gays and lesbians, the Palestinians and such like abandoned people around the world.

—God's third question every morning: *How shall I transmit these gifts to these folk?* And then God dispatches God's people with the gifts. God recruits gift-giving people into the church. That is why the church is a community of self-givers, the ones who refuse the *quid pro quo* of calculating, bargaining transactionalism. This is a community that does not ask, "What's in it for me?" because we have already received overwhelming free gifts from God. The church is a company of those designated by the gospel to deliver the goodness of the creator God in terms of mercy, compassion, forgiveness, generosity, hospitality, and restorative justice. Presbyterians instructed by John Calvin, moreover, know that one form of such generosity from God is to pay good, wise, and generous taxes that will bring wellbeing to those who are without resources.

It is our mandate as church to bring self-giving wellbeing into the world.

As I thought about the *quid pro quo* church in Luther's time and the *quid pro quo* world all around us, I thought of Paul's two questions to the church in Corinth:

What do you have that you did not receive?

Why then do you boast?

And then I thought of two other questions that we might be asking ourselves. They could be questions we ask ourselves at daybreak when we get up, before we brush our teeth. Here are questions for early in the morning that could frame our day of faithfulness:

What do you have that you did not receive?

Or more simply:

What have you received as a gift?

We might give any number of honest answers to that question. We have variously received in the goodness of God wealth or good health or good family or good work or a good education without any debt. Or a strong body or a community of good care or a deep love or a deep hope. It is all gift! It is all gift that we have not earned it and we don't act as though it is our accomplishment or possession.

The second question we may ask at daybreak is:

What gift might I give today of the gifts that have been given to me?

That might be a gift of my money or of my time or of a particular talent or skill set or any capacity for neighborliness or a political engagement for justice or a long term investment in the commonwealth or a letter or a prayer or a protest or a good word. These are all gifts we may give today that have transformative potential! If we do not ask questions like these, it is likely that we will, by default, go along with the anti-neighborly fear and greed of the world. If you want to participate in the on-going work of the Reformation that is not yet finished, pose these two questions:

What have I received today as a gift?

What might I give today?

We may position ourselves as a part of a gift-receiving, gift-giving world because God is a gift-giving God. We may live in the same world as Elisha who did free healing, what a thought . . . free health care! Or we could be bamboozled like the Syrian general who was dazzled by free health care, for he had never before received any such free gift.

When we live in a gift-receiving, gift-giving world, we don't need to belong to the dog-eat-dog world of greed, fear, and violence. We do not need to practice the conventional ways of greed, accumulation, and hoarding for ourselves. Remember, these two questions from Paul are in the same letter to the church in Corinth to whom he wrote the more familiar lyrical words of "a more excellent way":

> Love is patient; love is kind; love is not envious or boastful
> or arrogant or rude. It does not insist on its own way; it is
> not irritable or resentful; it does not rejoice in wrongdo-
> ing, but rejoices in the truth. It bears all things, believes
> all things, hopes all things, endures all things. Love never
> ends . . . And now faith, hope, and love abide, these three;
> and the greatest of these is love. (1 Cor 13:4–8, 13)

This is about being re-formed. That is what the Reformation is about, being *re-formed* after we have been *de-formed*. We have been deformed by the harsh powerful codes of fear, greed, and violence. Now the Spirit of God is at work re-forming us that we may become more fully who we truly are as God's good creatures. We are gift-receiving and gift-giving partners of God's endless flow of generosity that makes all things new.

Montview Blvd. Presbyterian Church
October 25, 2010

14

WE SING WHAT WE CANNOT SAY

AT A STUDY SESSION in our church, I was expositing biblical rhetoric whereby God is a real character and a lively agent who can intrude into the world in effective ways in order to create new futures. A friend of mine, a relentless "progressive," spoke up to say that she could never say such words that attribute such agency to God. She could not say such words because their claim clearly violates her Enlightenment reasonableness in her faith. (Thank goodness Methodists include "reason" in the "quadrilateral of authority.") But then it occurred to me that my friend sings in our church choir. She sings of angels at Christmas. She sings of a rising at Easter. She sings of the rush of the Spirit at Pentecost. She sings such claims without batting an eye. Then it occurred to me concerning my friend and all of us: "We sing what we cannot say." We sing such words and make such claims in our singing because lyrical poetic discourse that can tease, contradict, and exaggerate, is porous and elusive, and is not bound by the strict rules that govern and contain our prosaic speech. In what follows I will reflect on my recent learning that we sing what we dare not say. I will consider three dimensions of that singing.

∾

After a successful foray against the Philistines, the women in Israel welcomed their men home with singing:

> Saul has killed his thousands,
> and David his ten thousands. (1 Sam 18:7)

The first line of the song is celebrative of King Saul for his prowess against the Philistines! The song must have pleased the king. Or at least until he heard the second line of the song that credited David with ten times as many killings. What sounded at first like a salute to King Saul is in fact a set-up to make a bigger claim for his rival, David. When King Saul heard the second line of the song by the women he was angry, for he recognized the threat implied to his stature and position:

> Saul was very angry, for this saying displeased him. He said, "They have ascribed to David ten thousands, and to me they have ascribed thousands; what more can he have but the kingdom?" So Saul eyed David from that day on. (1 Sam 18:8–9)

Saul could do the numbers! The song that appears to be celebrative of King Saul is in fact a subversion of Saul's royal authority and an affirmation that David would be a more effective king. The women would not dare to say that, because it would be treasonable. But they could sing it! While the king is angry he would not charge the women with treason, because they were only singing, engaged in a clever move that covertly shifted loyalty from Saul to David.

We sing what we cannot say because it is too dangerous for saying. It is like that, for example, with many "Negro Spirituals" that sing of escape from slavery. Thus "Steal Away to Jesus" might sound pious to white ears but the "hidden transcript" concerns flight to the North.[1] The lines, however, do not say what the song expresses. Since it is sung and not said, it is possible to give

---

1. See Scott, *Domination and the Arts of Resistance: Hidden Transcripts.*

expression, even if barely so. The women in Israel shrewdly sensed what subversion was permissible.

~

In 1 Sam 2:1–10 Hannah sings in expectation of the son that the priest Eli has just promised her. Her song is not about the son who is to come, but about YHWH who will give, authorize, and empower her son. We learn from her song that there is no one like the Holy One of Israel (v. 2). Her song tells us of the ways in which YHWH is unlike every other God. This God has the capacity to overthrow all social arrangements. Thus God has the capacity to kill and bring to life. More specifically this God can reallocate the earth's food supply:

> Those who were full have hired themselves out for bread,
> but those who were hungry are fat with spoil. (v. 5)

Because this God is Lord of the rich and of the poor, this God with a preferential option for the poor can elevate the poor to places of power and elevate the needy to places of honor. This is nothing less than a social revolution.

The work of this God is at least subversive. More than that, it is revolutionary in a way that upends the status quo. One could hardly say that in places of power and authority; but one can sing it! We even sing in echo of Hannah in great cathedrals and on high holy days. It may be dangerous, but it is permissible because it is sung.

It is no wonder that this great revolutionary singing of Hannah is reiterated in the story of Jesus. For good reason, Luke has placed an echo of Hannah's song at the beginning of his gospel in the mouth of Mary. Luke, among the four evangelists, is the most radical in remembering Jesus as the one who signaled an immense upheaval in the socio-economic world. Thus Mary, in anticipation of the work of Jesus, sings to "magnify" the wonder of God (Luke 1:46–55). Mary sings of a "Mighty One" who, as with Hannah, can and will enact social upheaval in order to make the last ones first:

> He has brought down the powerful from their thrones,
>> and lifted up the lowly;
> he has filled the hungry with good things,
>> and sent the rich away empty. (vv. 52–53)

Such an articulation of God's "preferential option for the poor" soon is to be performed by Jesus is hardly palatable in many Christian congregations. But we can sing what we cannot say. We sing of a revolution that contradicts and threatens present world arrangements. In our singing we acknowledge this God who is free from and over against our preferred socio-economic policies and practices.

∼

Among the most lyrical words in the Bible is the poetry of Second Isaiah that anticipates Israel's coming return from exile in Babylon (Isaiah 40–55). Because that return from exile will challenge the still regnant Babylonian Empire, this expectation must be sung. This poetry is filled with ebullient expectation that invites Israel to anticipate beyond present political circumstance even though present political reality is daunting.

In Isa 42:10 Israel is summoned to sing a "new song," a never-before sung song before in Israel to point to a divine wonder that has never been seen before. The subject of that new song is the arousal and resilience of God who is daringly portrayed not unlike a pregnant woman who breaks the long silence of exile who now cries out:

> Now I will cry out like a woman in labor,
>> I will gasp and pant. (v. 14)

The imagery concerns the birthing of something new that is not derived from what has been. The newness concerns the lordly devastation of "nature":

> I will lay waste mountains and hills,
>> and dry up all their herbage;
> I will turn the rivers into islands,
>> And dry up the pools. (v. 15)

That disturbance of "nature," however, is in order to announce how YHWH will act to bring Israel home from exile:

> I will lead the blind by a road they do not know,
>> by paths they have not known I will guide them.
> I will turn the darkness before them into light,
>> the rough places into level ground.
> These are the things I will do,
>> and I will not forsake them. (v. 16)

That new song about new historical reality will question and delegitimate the Babylonian Empire. It would have been dangerous to say out loud that Babylon has reached the end of its imperial rule. But that is the claim of the song. It is doxology that anticipates well beyond the prosaic language of the empire that is characteristically the language of despair.

In Isa 54:1 exilic Israel is addressed by the imperative, "sing." We might expect that exilic Israel would say that it is much too dismayed to sing. The poetry, however, not only commands Israel to sing. The poetry tells Israel why it must now sing. The imperative is addressed to "barren Israel" with the imagery of a woman who has no children and no prospect for pregnancy (see Gen 11:30). This disappointed woman had no reason to sing or rejoice. Except now, by the imperative of God, this barren woman will give birth, receive futures, and will have more children, (a greater future) than the Babylonian Empire that had been so arrogant and is now fated to despair. History has turned! The exiles will have more of future wellbeing than anyone could have expected!

This barren hapless woman in exile, Israel, will have so many children, so much future, that she will need a bigger tent. The place will be crawling with children, so much so that the tent stakes and ropes will need to be reinforced to cope with the burgeoning population that will occupy the future. The summons is to sing in order to boast, celebrate, and acknowledge that hopeless Israel has a wondrous future because of the faithfulness of God. The counterpoint to be sung is that the empire has no children, that is, no future. Imagine a song to declare an empire is without a future! This is dangerous talk. It is always dangerous to anticipate a future that contradicts and overthrows present reality. Thus Israel is an anticipation of Martin Luther King's assurance, "I have a dream." It is a dream that overrides the present nightmare of displacement. The only way to do that is by singing. We might judge that this singing in exile is an early version of "We Shall Overcome." Long, loud, bold singing of that song was the prerequisite of its bold use by Lyndon Johnson as the conclusion to his earnest Civil Rights speech before Congress. It had to be sung long, loudly, and often. We sing because we anticipate that by the power of God all present social reality can be overthrown.

The furthest reach of such singing in the book of Isaiah is in 26:1–19. The poetry is introduced in this way:

> On that day this song will be sung in the land of Judah. (v.1)

There will be a time for singing. In that time there will be to a new wave of God's rule. But first the song must acknowledge that Israel was pregnant with possibility, only to fail:

> Like a woman with child,
>   who writhes and cries out in her pang
>   when she is near to her time,
> so were we because of you, O YHWH;
>   we were with child; we writhed,
>   but we gave birth only to wind.
> We have won no victories on earth,
>   and no one is born to inhabit the world. (vv. 17–18)

But then in v. 19 the song does a mighty reversal. Now Israel is to "Sing for joy."

> Your deed shall live,
>   their corpses shall rise.
> O dwellers in the dust,
>   awake and sing for joy! (v. 19)

At the edge of the Old Testament Israel sings that "dust" will be overcome; corpses will rise. This is Israel's ultimate anticipation. And if we consider that "dust" takes many forms including exile, poverty, greed, violence, and fear, it may mean anything lethal. The song of faithful Israel trusts that the God of life will override and reject the negating power of "dust." This is the ultimate song of Israel. Such faith cannot be said, for the flatness of prose will miss the celebrative joy and amazement of this stupendous claim. It must be sung! That is why our best singing is at Easter when we sing what we cannot say about God's power for life in every circumstance of death.

If we try to say our faith in the reasoned cadences of worldly logic, our best claims are empty and lifeless. Our gospel faith is *subversive, revolutionary and anticipatory*. But when it is said and not sung,

—Subversion becomes *conformity*,

—Revolution becomes *romantic nostalgia*, and

—Anticipation becomes *silent acquiescence to the status quo*.

Thus our work is to practice singing and to school the church in its singing.

But a caveat is in order. Many people in many Christian congregations are so inured to an anemic civic religion and so are narcoticized against the demanding, dangerous dimensions of our best singing so that its thickness goes unrecognized. It is necessary that pastors and other song leaders among the faithful must do the work of critical awareness that Paulo Freire has termed "conscientization."[2] Or in more popular expression, that we should be "woke." Without such critical awareness, the markers of *subversion, revolution, and anticipation* go unnoticed as we mouth the words. But think of it: our faithful singing is the embrace of *subversion, revolution, and anticipation* that bring life.

That is why we sign of angels at Christmas, governing messengers who make Herod quiver;

> That is why we sing at Easter,
> The strife of o'er, the battle done;
> The victory of life is won;
> The song of triumph has begun.[3]

2. Freire, *Pedagogy of the Oppressed*.

3. *Glory to God*, 236.

That is why we pray for breath at Pentecost in a society where we hear too often, "I can't breathe."

> Breath on me, breathe of God, fill me with life anew,
> That I may love what thou dost love, and do what thou
> wouldst do.[4]

That is why in glad obedience, we march in our faith, "Marching in the Light of God."[5]

Did you know that in 1985 the government of South Africa banned Christmas Carols in the townships?

> A candlelight procession along Cape Town's sea front by about 600 people, mostly whites, combining favorite carols and religious hymns with anti-apartheid songs and chants, was broken up by police using whips after they had declared it an "illegal gathering" and ordered the marchers to disperse within five minutes . . . Police, wielding long whips, fired tear-gas grenades and wrenching candles from the hands of participants, have broken up vigils all around Cape Town during the last month.[6]

Songs were said to be too "emotional." By that they meant *too subversive*, *too revolutionary*, and *too anticipatory*. Singing threatens the status quo when sung properly. We sing what we cannot say. When we say and do not sing, we end in despair that leads to violence and death. Happily my friend at church is fully "woke"!

4. *Glory to God*, 286.
5. *Glory to God*, 853. See Brueggemann, *A Glad Obedience*.
6. Parks, "S. Africa City Cracks Down on Christmas."

15

YOUNG MEN, YOUNG GIRLS,
FLOWERS . . . WHERE?

I TAKE THE LIBERTY of offering something of a book review; the book is published by a small press in my hometown of Traverse City (Mission Point Press) and might not be much noticed. It is titled *When Truth Mattered: The Kent State Shootings 50 Years Later* by Robert Giles.[1] It is a careful report and summary of the Kent State killings as covered by Akron, Ohio's *Beacon Journal*, owned by Knight Newspapers, "the best newspaper chain in the nation." The author, Giles, was the managing editor of the *Beacon Journal* at the time of the killings. The book not only offers a full account of the events on the Kent State campus, but is especially attentive to the work of journalists and the careful way in which they reported the happenings on campus, checked facts, and remained steadfastly objective in their reportage. With the executive editor, Ben Maidenburg, out of town, Giles was the man in charge. By the fluke of a single open phone line kept open by a cooperative staff person on campus, the *Beacon Journal* had singular access to the events of the day and a clear claim to do first-hand reporting that was not on offer to any other paper.

1. Giles, *When Truth Mattered.*

From Giles's compelling telling we may summarize the factors that served to evoke and produce the bloody outcome of May 4, 1970, on campus:

— The framing reality of the day was the aggressive action of President Nixon in Southeast Asia amid the Viet Nam War in his single-minded pursuit of "communists," a pursuit that was sure to inflame many students.

— Very quickly the Ohio governor, James Rhodes, took control of the campus, pushing aside any possible leadership by campus officials. Rhodes was in hot pursuit of a senate seat from Ohio and seized the opportunity to assume a "law and order" posture, and then engaged in inflammatory demagoguery to goad the process along.

— The National Guard, mobilized by Governor Rhodes, was ill-prepared for the occupation of the campus, appearing to one faculty observer "as scared to death . . . a bunch of summertime soldiers."[2] That ill preparation led to what turned out to be an unprovoked firing on defenseless students, as many as sixty-one bullets!

— The final ingredient was the moral passion of students on campus, dismayed by the cynical violence of Nixon policy, and no doubt alert to the prospect of the military draft. (Members of the university faculty were a stabilizing force amid the confusion.)

This convergence of factors, as is well known, lead to four student deaths (murders!), and derivatively to the legitimated habit of violence toward protesters.

We may notice three outcomes of that bloody failure of "law and order":

— The *Beacon Journal* won a Pulitzer Prize for its quite remarkable coverage, a hard-won prize that greatly delighted Giles and his staff.

2. Giles, *When Truth Mattered*, 117.

— The trial of four National Guardsmen who had fired on the students resulted in acquittal, a verdict that evoked huge negative response.

— The university eventually established a durable memorial on campus to the students. The memorial may be taken as a specific marker for the deep scar left by the gross state violence on the campus and on the larger national community.

The "truth" about which Giles writes is the truthfulness of good journalism that then and now plays a decisive role in the democratic processes of our society, a role unintimidated by frantic charges of "fake news." But the naming of "truth" also refers to the truth carried by the students in their moral passion against the violent power of the state. Giles dos not address this second level of truth because he is a journalist and not a preacher. Not surprisingly, when that "truth" meets such "power," power will characteristically prevail through violence. Except, of course, that the truth of the matter persists in, through, and beyond the violence.

I would not try too hard to relate this drama of truth and power in any close way to Scripture (as is my wont). But a biblical text that comes to me is the narrative of 2 Kgs 10:18–31. In this narrative the long-running dynasty of Omri and Ahab had been quite successful and was, perforce, full of religious compromise. An upstart, Jehu, had been anointed by Elisha to subvert the wayward dynasty and seize power in the name of radical Yahwism (2 Kgs 9:1–13). "Acting with cunning" (10:19), Jehu summoned his subjects—all prophets and all worshippers of Baal—to a great ceremony of sacrifice; he required everyone to show up:

> Let none be missing, for I have a great sacrifice to offer to Baal; whoever is missing shall not live. (v. 19)

Jehu put on a big exhibit of religious ostentation. But then when the required assembly was all gathered and secured, Jehu acted out his real intent and ordered the massacre of all of those who had come to the liturgy:

> Now Jehu had stationed eighty men outside, saying, "Whoever allows any of those to escape whom I deliver into your hands shall forfeit his life." As soon as he had finished presenting the burnt offering, Jehu said to the guards and to the officers, "Come in and kill them; let no one escape." So they put them to the sword. (vv. 24–26)

It required only "eighty men" to implement the killing that established the rule of Jehu that lasted twenty-eight years (10:34–36). Jehu received only a rote condemnation from the editors of the books of Kings with nothing negative said about the massacre he authorized (vv. 30–31)!

I cite this narrative because it is an account of a "pure" political vision (pure Yahwism!) that is able and willing to implement massive violence against those who resist or violate that ideology; the violence is a ready tool with which to seize and hold power. When the ideology is strong enough, it evidently justifies such violence against all who fail the pure ideology and engage in resistant conduct. Only a small number of the obediently willing is sufficient to advance the cause of the ideology and purge those who are resistant. When that small number of the obedient can act, then the beneficiaries of the ideology are secure and can prosper.

It will be clear, I assume, that my derivation from Giles's fine book is not simply because of an historical interest in the Kent State killings. Rather, as we are all aware, we have watched in 2019 something of a replay of this drama in the cities of Portland and Seattle (and elsewhere) where hosts of (mostly young) protestors have been assaulted by unidentified troops that have acted at the behest of the federal government (without invitation from local officials). These troops appear to be designed to advance "law and order" ideology in the interest of particular political futures. The analogue between the Kent State killings and our current situation need not be drawn too closely to see that yet again we are witnessing the *truth of moral passion* in the face of *the power of the state* that is propelled by the ideology of nationalism with unmistakable racist overtones. We can see the ingredients of Kent State reperformed:

— Nixon then had "communism" and now Trump has "nationalism" with the protection of federal property.

— Governor Rhodes was then the great demagogic leader, a role now willingly occupied by the president who is greatly skilled at inflammatory rhetoric.

— Instead of an ill-prepared National Guard we had then, we now have a variety of unidentified federal troops who are equally ill-prepared for the task to which they are assigned, an ill preparation that seems a warrant for violence linked to nervous triggers.

— Now as then we witness great moral passion expressed by protesters concerning ill-advised policy, in our present case permeated with racism, a moral passion rooted deeply in the great legacy of our national identity.

The ingredients are all present among us for a re-performance of that which Giles has so carefully reported. It will be clear to any reader that Bob Giles is not in any way implicated in my extrapolations from his important book concerning his excellence as a journalist.

Back in the days of Kent State and Viet Nam, Pete Seeger left us with the urgent unanswered question, "When will they ever learn?"

Where have all the flowers gone? . . .
Where have all the young girls gone? . . .
Where have all the young men gone? . . .
Where have all the soldiers gone? . . .
Where have all the graveyards gone? . . .
    Oh, when will they ever learn? . . .

Maybe now is a time for learning! That will not happen, however, without bold, intentional reliable teachers.

BIBLIOGRAPHY

Anderson, Bernhard W. *From Creation to New Creation: Old Testament Perspectives*. Overtures to Biblical Theology. Philadelphia: Fortress, 1994.

Barth, Karl. *Church Dogmatics III/1: The Doctrine of Creation, Part 1.* Edited by G. W. Bromiley and T. F. Torrance. Translated by J. W. Edwards et al. Edinburgh: T. & T. Clark, 1958.

Brueggemann, Walter. *A Glad Obedience: Why and What We Sing.* Louisville: Westminster John Knox, 2019.

———. "Refusing the Bramble." In *Resisting Denial, Refusing Despair: And Other Essays*, 27–32. Eugene, OR: Cascade Books, 2020.

———. *Resisting Denial, Refusing Despair: And Other Essays*, 27–32. Eugene, OR: Cascade Books, 2020.

———. *Solomon: Israel's Ironic Icon of Human Achievement.* Studies on Personalities of the Old Testament. Columbia: University of South Carolina Press, 2005.

———. *Testimony to Otherwise: The Witness of Elijah and Elisha.* St. Louis: Chalice, 2001.

Cagaptay, Soner. *Erdogan's Empire: Turkey and the Politics of the Middle East.* New York: Tauris, 2020.

Caparros, Martin. *Hunger: The Oldest Problem.* Rev. ed. Brooklyn: Melville House, 2019.

Freire, Paolo. *Pedagogy of the Oppressed.* New York: Herder & Herder, 1970.

Giles, Robert. *When Truth Mattered: The Kent State Shootings 50 Years Later.* Traverse City, MI: Mission Point Press, 2020.

Glory to God: The Presbyterian Hymnal. Louisville: Westminster John Knox, 2013.

Graeber, David. *Debt: The First 5,000 Years.* Updated ed. Brooklyn: Melville House, 2014.

Lehmann, Paul. *The Transfiguration of Politics: The Presence and Power of Jesus of Nazareth in and over Human Affairs.* New York: Harper & Row, 1975.

Lohfink, Norbert. *The Great Themes from the Old Testament.* Translated by Ronald Walls. Chicago: Franciscan Herald, 1982.

Longfellow, Henry Wadsworth. "The Village Blacksmith." In *Ballads and Other Poems*. 3rd ed. Cambridge, UK: Owen, 1842.

Mantel, Hilary. *Bring Up the Bodies*. Wolf Hall Trilogy 2. New York: Holt, 2013.

————. *The Mirror and the Light*. Wolf Hall Trilogy 3. New York: Holt, 2020.

McBride, S. Dean. "Polity of the Covenant People: The Book of Deuteronomy." *Interpretation* 41 (1987) 229–44.

Miller, Patrick D. *The Ten Commandments*. Interpretation: Resources for the Use of Scripture in the Church. Louisville: Westminster John Knox, 2009.

O'Connor, Flannery. *Collected Stories*. Edited by Sally Fitzgerald. New York: Library of America, 1988.

Parks, Michael. "S. Africa City Cracks Down on Christmas: Caroling Banned as 'Emotional': Church Services Restricted." *Los Angeles Times*, Dec. 25, 1985.

Ringe, Sharon. *Jesus, Liberation, and the Biblical Jubilee: Images for Ethics and Christology*. Overtures to Biblical Theology. 1985. Reprint, Eugene, OR: Wipf & Stock, 2004.

Scott, James C. *Domination and the Arts of Resistance: Hidden Transcripts*. New Haven: Yale University Press, 1990.

Weapons of the Weak: Everyday Forms of Peasant Resistance, Domination and the Arts of Resistance—Hidden Transcripts. New Haven: Yale University Press, 1985.

United Methodist Hymnal. Nashville: Abingdon, 1989.

SCRIPTURE INDEX

INDEX OF NAMES

Made in United States
Troutdale, OR
07/16/2023

11304733R00076